# IT'S TIME TO WAKE UP NOW

# IT'S TIME TO WAKE UP NOW
## The Top Ten Myths that Can Hijack Spiritual Awakening
### by Don Oakley

Gold Star Publishing, Inc.

Gold Star Publishing, Inc.
376 Well Being Circle
Tazewell, TN 37879

Copyright © 2016 by Don Oakley

All rights reserved. No part of this book may be used or reproduced without prior written permission.

Published 2016

ISBN 978-0-9971565-4-6

Cover photograph © iStockPhoto.com/Grytsaj
Cover and book design by Susan Kurtz Graphics

Printed by CreateSpace, An Amazon.com Company

Available from Amazon.com and other retail outlets

# Contents

Acknowledgments / vii
Introduction / ix

> Myth #10
> Awakening Is Only for Religious People / 1
>
> Myth #9
> I Have to Be More Present / 25
>
> Myth #8
> It Takes Lifetimes to Undo All My Bad Karma / 49
>
> Myth #7
> I Have to Purify Myself First / 61
>
> Myth #6
> I Must Transcend All Thought / 79
>
> Myth #5
> I Have to Meditate—a Lot / 107
>
> Myth #4
> I Need to Get Rid of My Ego / 129
>
> Myth #3
> Cool Spiritual Experiences Are Evidence of My Progress / 151
>
> Myth #2
> Awakening Is an Achievement / 163
>
> Myth #1
> I Know What Awakening Will Look Like / 181

About the Author / 197
Suggested Further Reading / 199

# Acknowledgments

I am deeply grateful for everyone I have encountered in any way in this lifetime.

I am particularly indebted to Eckhart Tolle, who retrieved me from spiritual malaise, and to Adyashanti, without whose guidance and clarity I might not have found my way home.

I am very grateful for David Michelson's valuable review and comments which significantly enriched the book's scope.

I value and appreciate Susan Kurtz's support and talent in the design of this book.

And, finally, I am immensely grateful to my wife and co-journeyer, Patty Bottari, for her steadfast encouragement, for her patience, for her honest evaluations of earlier inept drafts, and for her unconditional love during the process.

# Introduction

Enlightenment can't be avoided forever. By all evidence, it can be avoided for a very long time, but not forever. Eventually, you will notice what you already are.

So the question is not *if,* but *when.*

This book is intended to hasten "when" by exposing misleading myths and outright fallacies about awakening that have evolved in the West over the last half century. Any one of these myths, if believed, has the power to hijack your whole spiritual search, take you for an unfruitful ride, and leave you stranded far from home. You can spend years or even decades in a barren desert with the mirage of awakening flickering alluringly on some distant horizon. Perhaps you have been a cooperative, if innocent, victim of just such a hijacking.

This book will help you see through the Top Ten of the most common and seductive myths about awakening. There are others, of course, but if you really get these Top Ten, you should have little trouble seeing through others that may arise as your mind tries desperately to remain in charge.

Many people believe that awakening is a path of more: more knowledge, more effort, more dogmas, more good deeds, more meditation, more ritual, etc. Others believe it is a path of otherworldly attainments and mystical revelations. Some even believe it is a path of bodily and worldly deprivation. Pursuit of these activities may be noble in intent, and perhaps even beneficial to the world at large, but may not ultimately improve your chances of enlightenment.

It all comes down to what you truly want. It's your choice, and there are no wrong answers. If you want a lifelong hobby, a nicely polished spiritualized identity, the comfort of certainty, and the companionship of fellow believers, there are plenty of suitable books out there for you. This is not one of them. However, if your intent is to awaken, then this book might just save you years of looking for enlightenment where it's not to be found.

The underlying assumption of these myths about awakening is that you lack something and you must go somewhere or do something to get it. To buy into this assumption, you must first deny your fully-present, as-is divinity so that you can run off in search of it. Truth is not something "out there" or something to be gained in the future after you've proven yourself worthy; it is what you already are—just here, right this moment, only awaiting recognition. It is hidden where you least expect to find it. We don't notice it because we are looking elsewhere. We expect it to be difficult, obscure, learned, otherworldly, or mind-blowing. Our minds love complexity. The universe obliges. And we go on seeking.

Spiritual awakening is not something to attain because you cannot attain what you already are. I am not talking about the "you" that you think you are, but rather that which *you really are.* Unavoidably. Right now. As is—as surprising as that is.

However, if you don't know that for yourself to your own unshakable satisfaction in your own moment-to-moment experience, or if you only believe it as a concept, it is of no lasting benefit. Since enlightenment is preexisting, the journey is to strip away everything that obscures it. And I'm not talking about self-improvement; I'm talking about seeing through false beliefs about, well . . . just about everything. Spiritual awakening is a path of unknowing what you think you already know including even your most cherished beliefs—even the beliefs about yourself and the world that are so ingrained that you don't even know you're carrying them.

Believing is not the same as knowing. Belief is what you think might be true, what you hope might be true, what you imagine might be true, what you fear might be true, or what you have been conditioned to think is true. But you don't *know* if it's actually true. In the awakening game, belief is like Kryptonite.

You might ask yourself right now, "What do

I know with absolute certainty right now in my own direct experience?" If you look deeply and are honest with yourself, it will be a very short list. In fact, if there is more than about one thing on your list, I suggest you summon up the courage to look more deeply. Not-knowing is an excellent place to start, especially if that's what's true.

There is no need to try to attain enlightenment directly. You'll try, of course, because it's so enticing, but waking up doesn't happen by frontal assault. Just eliminate what is falsely believed. When everything untrue is seen through, Truth remains. Truth (or Consciousness, the Infinite, Wholeness, or God—pick one that resonates for you) is the one treasure that cannot be destroyed by moths, or rust or by thieves as St. Matthew points out. Jed McKenna says: "Truth is the one thing that is not a belief." Ramana Maharshi teaches: "Let what comes, come. Let what goes, go. Find out what remains." *A Course in Miracles* informs us on the first page: "Nothing real can be threatened. Nothing unreal exists. Herein lies the peace of God."

It is called enlightenment because you are relieved of a burden you don't even know you're carrying. (If it were something added to you, it would have to be called "enheavyment.")

Seeking enlightenment is a journey only a fool would willingly take. If begun, there will come a point when it is too late to turn back to your old way of life. If you follow the path to its destination, it will cost you everything, you will receive nothing, and you will marvel at the bargain.

It is there now, waiting with infinite patience for you to drop all pretenses for just an instant and recognize the enormity of what you are.

My prayer is that this book will relieve you of misleading beliefs, save you years of aimless wandering, and leave you grace-prone to awaken.

You've been dreaming long enough, my friend. It's time to wake up now.

Be Well.

Don Oakley
May 2016

# Myth #10

"Awakening Is Only for Religious People"

Some religions advertise that they know the fast track to Nirvana; some claim to be the only track; some claim to know the secret path; some claim that there is no path.

We have been taught to believe, or we assume, that awakening is rare and reserved for special, pre-designated, divine souls. The consequence of this belief is that the rest of us are relegated to worshipping the awakened ones and perhaps making gradual changes to our second-class selves, aka "self-improvement." At best, we are told, we can only hope to honor the awakened ones and to try to mimic them to some limited degree.

There are several reasons for this myth to be so commonly, and unconsciously, accepted. First, of course, is that religions want their founders to be seen as unique and special compared with the rest of humanity—in advertising, they call that "branding." Secondly, of all the hundreds of thousands (probably millions) of people that have pursued enlightenment through the centuries, very few are commonly acknowledged to have arrived. Of course, we never hear about all those who had the good sense to remain quiet about their awakening. (After all, exuberant claims of enlightenment in the not too distant past often shortened one's life expectancy.) And thirdly, the belief that awakening is rare and for only a select few divine souls is consistent with the widespread belief that we are essentially unworthy. For some unfathomable reason, we (especially those of us who grew up in the West) were tainted at birth with "original sin" by an otherwise loving God. (Huh?)

It all adds up. It seems to make sense. It seems reasonable to conclude that enlightenment must be extremely rare—maybe even impossible—and, in any event, probably only for religious people, and certainly not even thinkable for someone as unworthy as I!

After all, how many people do you personally know whose birth was announced by a white elephant or who emerged from a lotus blossom or bore some such sign of divinity? Such events, as diligently reported by devoted followers, are no doubt sufficient proof of their founder's specialness. But what about the rest of us who were born surrounded by people wearing masks, held naked upside down, spanked, vaccinated, and given powdered formula to drink? There's not much there for some future marketing department to work with!

We all like to think that the founder of our own chosen religion is special; not just special, but truly divine—a cut above us mere humans. And we get to take home the consolation prize which is "I may not be divine, but at least I'm playing for the right team and I get to attend the after-game party."

Believing that awakening is limited to a few select, divine individuals is equivalent to believing that the rest of us are fundamentally flawed and unworthy of such a grand gift. We might conclude that there was a Grace lottery, and our number didn't come up. Or worse, "Maybe God doesn't like me." (That was one of my personal favorites for more years than I am willing to admit in print.)

Don't we all have sufficient evidence of our unworthiness?

- "My father told me that I was too shy to ever amount to much."
- "My mother said that her pregnancy was 'an accident.'" (Ouch!)
- "My elementary school teacher made fun of my stutter."
- "The basketball coach said I was too short."
- "The track coach said I was too slow."

- "My girlfriend said I was too fast."

I'm sure you can personalize the rant.

By the time we reach adulthood, it's astonishing that we don't lapse into prolonged episodes of unworthy despair at the slightest provocation. Or maybe we do. So if we feel this way about ordinary life as an adult, how can we possibly believe that we're even eligible for the "ultimate prize" of awakening?

Do you see how common tinges of unworthiness contribute to our logical and casual dismissal of the possibility of awakening in this lifetime?

We never question whether worthiness even enters into it.

What if it didn't? I mean it. What if worthiness just didn't factor into it—at all?

Being able to read this book means that you are alive and therefore inherently awake. No specialness required. You may not know this for yourself, but it's true. (Then again, knowing it yourself makes all the difference. It may be true, but if you haven't yet experienced the magnitude your inheritance, it is of little lasting benefit.)

My suggestion is to admit that you don't actually know if worthiness is a criterion. If so, be honest with yourself and at least allow the possibility that it may not be.

One of the ways that the Universe apparently works is that you get to experience what you believe. So, if you believe that awakening is only for special, divine souls (i.e., someone other than you), the Universe obligingly responds: "And so shall it be."

However, awakening is not reserved for "special, divine people." It's everyone's essential nature—as is. Awakening is just the realization of what you already are, as illogical as that seems to be. Worthiness doesn't factor into it. From our judgmental human minds, I know this doesn't make sense, but (fortunately) we don't get to make the rules.

Instead of feeling unworthy, maybe you feel entitled—one of the chosen few by virtue of membership in a particular religion or group. It's not even necessary to have a lot of people who believe the same thing to qualify as a religion as I'm defining it. You can have a religion of one person—yourself! As long as you have a fixed set of beliefs and insist on the truth of those beliefs and deny the possible validity of all others, you get to wear the religious button—either in the privacy of your own home or "on your sleeve" out in public. If you already stand in the certainty of your beliefs, you are no longer questioning your assumptions, and you are free to devote all your energy in the defense (or promotion) of your foregone conclusions. And you might even have centuries of co-believers to back you up! This seems to work for a lot of people, and that's fine—everyone gets a ticket at birth to make one's own choices.

Maybe you're a clever person and claim that God (Christ Consciousness, Buddha Nature, Yahweh, Allah, the One, Existence, the Infinite Potential, or whatever name you prefer) doesn't exist. But in order to claim that God does not exist, you must be alive and conscious. (If you are not conscious, you are unable to claim anything!) So then, please answer the question, "What is aware of my opinion that God does not exist?" If your answer is consciousness, can you describe that consciousness? Can you know with absolute certainty that the consciousness you sense is a function of the mass of brain cells in your head, or rather, might it be more true to say that consciousness is aware of the thoughts flickering through those brain cells? Has that consciousness changed over your lifetime, or has it always been there, noticing what was happening everywhere you happened to be? (Remember, I'm not talking about the content of the consciousness; I'm just talking about the nature of subjective consciousness itself.) In your own direct experience, does that consciousness extend only to the boundary of your scalp, or does it seem to extend out past the limits of your head? When you look around the room does it take in the whole room? How about the stars at night? Does consciousness have a form? Does it have a shape or is it more like spaciousness? You are your own authority. You get to call it as you see it. Just answer from your own present-time experience—not just from mental concepts.

OK. Let's sum up. Presuming your answers were thoughtful and honest, you may have concluded that this everyday consciousness is eternal, formless, limitless, and has a certain sense of aliveness to it. You get to call that spacious awareness anything you want—or better yet, not call it anything at all.

As a third alternative, you may find yourself straddling the fence: the "I don't know" path. It has been called "agnostic," which is Greek for "it's too soon for me to place any bets one way or the other." You might not think this qualifies as much of a path, but, in fact, it may be the most honest path out there. Because until you've looked really, really, really deeply—until you've doubted everything, until you've turned over every rock of your belief system to find out what lies underneath—the truth is that you don't *know*. It's not possible to believe your way to awakening. You get there by seeing through every belief you've ever adopted. You can do this one by one (the hard way), or you can see through the very nature of belief itself (the significantly more efficient way). Despite all logic to the contrary, recognizing the simple fact that you do not know anything of any ultimate importance is actually an excellent place to start your journey—simply because it is true. If you think you know something already, it is recommended that you back up, look more closely, and start at the beginning. Build your foundation on solid ground—no matter how tiny that toe hold may, at first, appear.

These days, a lot of people like to rely on science. In the last few centuries, many people have grown to trust science more than religion for answers to the "big" questions. Science has fueled our Industrial Age, built our cities, and created our techie gadgets. We now "know" that matter is made of atoms, and if we've read anything containing the word "quantum," we understand that atoms are made up of even smaller, flimsier bits of energy flitting in and out of existence. This raises questions about things we commonly trust, like chairs. A chair is something solid enough to sit on. However, from the perspective of an individual atom, the closest adjacent atom is far away: like grapefruits at either end of a football field. And those atoms are not themselves solid and may be mere patterns of energy that are in turn affected by the consciousness of the observer. This is not philosophy; this is what our best particle physicists are telling us. What looks solid to us at our human scale of perception may be no more substantial than an energetic fog and consciousness (our observations) can apparently alter the nature of that fog. (Hmm... consciousness altering matter—we may be more powerful than we ever imagined!)

Then there is the issue of Dark Matter and Dark Energy, which are semi-dignified terms physicists use to refer to mysterious, overwhelmingly massive attributes of the Universe rather than saying, "Hey folks, we don't have a clue what ninety-six percent of the Universe actually is." Wait a minute . . . what's going on here? Physics is getting weirder and more mystical. Scientists keep promising that they are on the verge of discovering a unified theory of everything, but so far, frontier science keeps drifting into the "Unknowable."

Are you really willing to leave it to science to tell you what your place in the cosmos is? Before you answer that question, you might ask yourself whether it makes sense to worship at the same altar that has genetically modified our food, poisoned our honeybee pollinators, and put neurotoxins in our childhood vaccines. Maybe it's just me, but it doesn't seem like science has this Oneness-of-All-Life thing quite figured out yet.

On an even more mundane, everyday level, does anybody know why we feel rested after sleeping for eight hours, even though we do it every night? Or how a plant uses sunlight to grow? (Nope. Sorry. Just assigning symbols to chemical reactions doesn't count.) Or what happens at the moment of death? Or where selfless love comes from? Or what a fresh fig tastes like if you've never tasted one? We can experience these mysteries, but we can't explain them in any satisfactory way. Words fall flat.

What is real is beyond the capacity of concepts to convey. Awakening to Truth is beyond the confinement of conceptual thought.

Sure, there are plenty of things we can know. We can learn to read and write and type with our thumbs, build a house, solve an algebra problem, or learn the formula for Coca-Cola®. And that's all fine and useful in order to earn a living and to get by in this world. But that's not the kind of knowing that we're talking about.

So, if we are willing to be honest with ourselves and start from a place of naked unknowing, we might first ask ourselves, if only God exists, where shall I seek?

Good question.

Any attempt to go on a search for God seems

to deny God's presence right here and now. And yet, unless you get the full implication of that statement, you have to start somewhere.

Some religious people wake up. Some non-religious people do too. Remember: Jesus was not a Christian, and Buddha was not a Buddhist. Religions tend to coalesce around an awakened (or sometimes, unfortunately, simply a charismatic) leader. The codification that follows often dampens the original flame of enlightened perception. Over time, formalized beliefs are adopted because they are easier to disseminate and offer more efficient control of the flock. They are also easier to embellish. Truth cannot be embellished because it cannot be condensed into words, and there is no belief to embellish. Of course people try, but it cannot be improved upon. When anyone tries to reduce it to words, the only question is the degree of distortion. If the conversion into concepts is not too distorted, it may be helpful—it still won't be Truth, but it may be helpful.

Truth is just the astonishingly ordinary, unbelievably stunning, ever-present potential of Life unfolding in silence endlessly. Without the words. And not even that.

Religion, on the other hand, is a set of written, formalized beliefs. Many religions advertise that if their unique set of beliefs is believed, spiritual benefits will be bestowed on the believer. It is no doubt an enormous relief when you can adopt a set of ready-made beliefs that will put all life's uncertainties to rest. And that is totally fine. When I think about the world, I am happy that most religions teach people to be kind to each other, to help the needy, and to try to avoid killing each other. If you are going to have beliefs to live by, these are certainly better than most.

Of course, trying to be good for too long can be tiresome, and, historically religions have had to take intermissions from time to time to go on jihads, fight crusades, root out infidels, engage in ethnic cleansings, hold inquisitions, or fight my-god versus your-god wars. Presumably, these activities are undertaken to convince opponents to be more loving to each other and to impart the cherished principle of Oneness to non-believers. Say what?

But what if awakening only happens beyond thought, which by definition, is also beyond all belief? Where's the religion in that?

It is astonishing to realize that awakening (enlightenment) is not religious—it's not even spiritual! Imagine that! No, really, I mean it. Take a moment to ponder that enlightenment might not be spiritual or religious.

To say that awakening is spiritual divides Life into two realms: spiritual and worldly. But the only God I'm interested in talking about is the God of the whole, not the assistant god whose kingdom is only a portion of existence, i.e., the spiritual portion. If, however, it is indeed all One, is it spiritual or is it non-spiritual? Or does this distinction just collapse when viewed from the perspective of Oneness?

If everything in the world were exactly the same hue of orange, no one would say "Orange is my favorite color" or "Orange is such a spiritual color." If it's the only "thing" that exists, it is neither spiritual nor special. It just *is*. Awakeness is like that.

A warning: If you ever encounter someone who has had some awakening experience and therefore considers himself/herself to be special—run very fast! A half-enlightened ego caught in the belief trap of specialness is dangerous. If that person also happens to be charismatic, then he/she is doubly dangerous. (Examples of this phenomenon are too numerous to require mention.)

Believing that you are not special enough before awakening is a false barrier; believing you are special compared to others after awakening is delusional.

When Buddha was asked what he had gained from supreme enlightenment, he reportedly said, "I have gained absolutely nothing." He wasn't being modest, folks; he was telling the truth as seen from the perspective of awakeness. Awakeness is what is left after the false is peeled away. He recognized that he didn't achieve anything. No thing was gained. Or, if you prefer, *nothing* was gained. He recognized what he had always been and what others already (unknowingly) are.

If you are pursuing enlightenment for your own aggrandizement, you will be either deluded or disappointed. It's not what you gain; it's what you lose. Truth is already present. It is obscured only by your belief in what is not true. And all beliefs are false.

It seems logical to believe that a belief in God or some divine being is a necessity when one goes looking to find Divinity. "Shouldn't that be a prerequisite to awakening?" But, come on. Do you really think Wholeness requires our puny on-again, off-again belief—yea or nay—in order to exist? Either Truth exists, or it does not. However, to state unequivocally that Truth does not exist requires a consciousness that can discern the difference, which means that Truth can be recognized and therefore exists. If Truth exists and if its domain is infinite, then untruth cannot actually exist (as it might in some hyper-theoretical alternative Universe). Untruth is just confusion existing as another manifestation of Truth within Oneness. Confusion, by the way, is not sinful; it is just ignorance. This is the non-dual perspective, or as Ramana Maharshi called it, "One without a second."

You either know something with certainty or you have not yet inquired deeply enough. In the awakening game, it is critical to be clear which is which. In between is the purgatory of belief. A belief is something that you don't know firsthand, but that you want to believe anyway because believing it is pleasant and convenient. Or you believe it because you are too lazy or hazy to question it. However, wishful thinking is not conducive to awakening.

If you look up and see the sun, you don't say, "I believe it's a sunny day." You just report simply, "It's a sunny day" because you were outside, and that's what you personally witnessed. There is no doubt. You had a direct experience of the sun. On the other hand, imagine you have been blind from birth. People may have told you that the warmth on your skin means the sun is shining, but you can't say for sure yourself what the sun looks like or even if the sun is what was producing the sensation of warmth. In which case, you can only say honestly, "I don't know for sure whether or not it's a sunny day. People tell me it is, and that might be true, but I cannot say with certainty for myself." This is just simple clarity about what you know from direct experience and what you don't know. It's your most fundamental tool in the awakening game.

You can't awaken by believing, hoping, acting, imagining, or faking your way there. You have to do the heavy lifting yourself. No guru is going to do it for you. A guru might point you in the right direction, or get you high, or maybe help you peek behind the curtain, but ultimately, you have to walk down the path to nowhere all by yourself. Did you really think it would be otherwise?

Beliefs, judgments, and opinions—even spiritual ones—are the Sirens of non-awakeness. They posture as Truth. They may, at best, be relatively true, but they are never absolutely true.

It is relatively true that it is a good idea to drive on the right hand side of the road—except when you are in England, when it is not. Life is complex. Relative truths depend on the situation. "Thou shalt not kill," but if you are a schoolteacher with the means to stop a rampaging murderer, I suggest that intervention may be appropriate. These are relative truths.

If we use the terms "God" and "Truth" interchangeably (which I do) and if there is indeed only one thing happening, then there is only one absolute Truth. That Truth can never be reduced to a catchy phrase or even into a scholarly treatise. Any attempt to do so is doomed from the start. Lao Tzu starts off the *Tao Te Ching* by confessing, "The Tao that can be spoken is not the true Tao." And then he proceeds with the attempt. Similarly, Adyashanti likes to say that his "job is to fail well."

Why is it impossible to reduce Truth into words? Because words are concepts *about* Truth (at best) and concepts about reality are no more than man-made fabrications. Truth contains infinite possibilities. A finite concept will never encompass it. Not ever. Not in the past. Not in the future. You cannot say what Truth is. You can't even think about it.

Scott Kiloby: "Looking out into the world, everything is happening in that seeing space. To point to your natural state, we use words that describe the absence of something including timelessness, formlessness, silence, nonconceptual awareness, and selflessness. Don't get caught up in the words. They are merely pointing you to this seeing space, the space in which time, form, sound, concepts, self and everything else arises."

So, back to the original question: is religion a prerequisite for awakening? Well, religious orientation may be helpful for many people, but it is not necessary to awaken because awakening is beyond mind and beyond all concepts and beliefs. For many people, such as Fred Davis, Scott Kiloby, and Byron Katie, the journey led through intoxicants. For others, such as Eckhart Tolle, the abject suffering of depression preceded awakening. Sometimes the death of a loved one, or one's own terminal illness, can focus attention like nothing else. And then, some people are just drawn to the search for no apparent reason. Or maybe you have simply run out of pathways promising happiness to run down expectantly.

What is perhaps more important than the particulars of the path or one's brand of religion is one's own intensity, honesty, and courage. When asked what is the most important attribute to awaken, Nisargadatta responded, "Earnestness." No path has a lock on these noble attributes. At the end of every true path, you find yourself alone. In that place, only these innate attributes are of any real help. Practice with small challenges, so that you are prepared when major opportunities present themselves.

Be foolhardy and dare to step naked into the unknown domain of your own existence. No worries. After all, what is true cannot be lost. And what is false is not real.

In the end, there is no "other." It's all One, and you are not separate in any way from that One Existence.

But don't take my word (or anyone else's word) for it. Only *you* can step beyond the mind into Truth.

Be intense in your search.

Be honest with yourself about what you know and what you don't know.

Be earnest and live what you realize.

Be courageous. Keep going when fear is present—especially when fear is present.

Be grateful when you have been graced by good fortune. Even better, just be grateful.

Avoid complacency and journey on!

Awake and enjoy letting let Life live you.

# Myth #9

"I Have to Be More Present"

Most of us have read Ram Dass' book *Remember: Be Here Now,* which inspired a generation of spiritual seekers. I have a lot of respect for Ram Dass. He was an early Eastern explorer venturing into dangerous unknown territory, and he's been open and honest about his very public journey for the last half century.

However, what most of us took away from *Remember: Be Here Now* was that we had to try really, really hard to be more present to the present moment. And perhaps, if we could be fully present all the time, we would get enlightened. (Or maybe it was the other way around: if we were awake, we would be fully present all the time. I don't remember.) In any event, the words "Remember: Be Here Now" were catchy and, therefore, memorable.

However, all teachings are only appropriate at a particular point in one's journey. No teaching is the right teaching for everyone all of the time. At one point effort is needed; at another point, letting go may be the path. To try to be more present to what is actually happening at any moment in one's life, is a useful, but limited, teaching. It is useful if you just want to slow down, get "centered," and gain a little balance in your life.

However, it can be a limiting teaching if one holds onto it too long. Why?

First of all, the commandment to "Be Here Now" assumes that it is possible to exist somewhere other than Here and at some time other than Now. Secondly, this phrase implies that the effort of remembering is required to keep these Mind Body Units (MBUs) in the here and now;

otherwise, presumably, they would go spinning out of orbit into the "there and then." And thirdly, the directive to "Be Here Now" suggests that spiritual benefits of high order will be ours if we can succeed in this self-conscious exercise.

But are any of these underlying assumptions actually true, or did we just adopt them like the cute puppy in the window? Is making an effort to be present to this powerful Now necessary and beneficial, or is it just another thing to add to my spiritual "To Do" list? We should not be deterred from asking valid questions even of our modern spiritual giants.

Religions tell us that belief is necessary and good, and that doubt is a weakness and a barrier on our journey to find God. Remember Doubting Thomas? One moment of reasonable doubt two thousand years ago and people are still talking about it. But the awakening process is not necessarily religious, although it can be approached in those terms. In the enlightenment game, doubt is your friend. Question everything; believe nothing. It is the beliefs that we don't know we've adopted that are the most dangerous. René Decartes counseled, "If you would be a real seeker after truth, it is necessary that at least once in your life to doubt, as far as possible, all things."

So let's question whether it's necessary and beneficial to remember to Be Here Now.

OK, I'll go first. Is it necessary or beneficial to try hard to remember to be present?

The command "Remember" implies effort. Every time we forget to "Be Here Now," it feels like we've fallen off the spiritual wagon. In fact, even after forty years of trying to be present, it can feel like we spend way more time off the wagon than on it.

This can be especially obvious when we sit down to meditate. We keep getting lost in thought, and then, occasionally and spontaneously, we come back into a more spacious awareness. When we do, we often have the thought, "Oh, I've been lost in thought for the last twenty minutes," and then we punish ourselves ("bad meditator, bad"). However, self-flagellation when we "come to" after daydreaming is just backwards. Ask any animal trainer. It's no way to train a restless beast like the human mind. It seems like gratitude is more appropriate than punishment when awareness returns to the foreground. Who knows? Without some element of grace, we could have remained lost in thought for the rest of our lives—many people do; instead, we "spontaneously" come back to awareness. Be grateful.

In fact, for those who find guidelines helpful, that's a decent one: when in doubt, be grateful. Gratitude is a pretty darn good, all-around, general-purpose, default setting. I'd even wager that if you could remain in a state of total gratitude for just twenty-four hours—I mean resting in utter gratitude for everything that's ever happened to you, for your own shortcomings, for that ex-boyfriend, for your parents or lack thereof, for your boss, and for everything that could ever happen to you in the future—awakening would be nearly unavoidable.

Noticing with gratitude when we occasionally become present is one thing, but making our life about trying to be present all the time is something else altogether. The first is effortless; it is a blessing when it happens, and it allows consciousness to flow as it will—sometimes expansive, sometimes focused; sometimes blissful, sometimes contracted. Sometimes consciousness is conscious of itself, and sometimes it is conscious of a thought-stream or a bird in flight. It just seems to be how things flow when they are allowed to be as they are. The task of remembering, on the other hand, requires effort to try to corral consciousness and it fosters a sense of unworthiness when we "fail" (which we invariably do time and time again).

Don't we have enough self-inflicted and largely unattainable goals in our lives already? Do we really need one more?

I realize that some long-time meditators have become skillful at repressing thought and are able to remain present while sitting for long periods.

However, is that what you set out to do years ago when you started meditating—to get really good at sitting quietly by yourself in a room? Didn't your meditation goals include freedom from perceived limitations? Freedom to experience life fully? Freedom to be authentically yourself? If freedom happens only when you are sitting undisturbed in a quiet room, that's a nice break, but how free is that, really? What happens when you get up off the cushion and go downstairs to join the fam or drive to work in traffic? How well does your spaciousness hold up then? I think it was even Ram Dass who first said, "If you think you're enlightened, spend a weekend with your parents."

Enlightenment, as the Taoists point out, is effortless—the Way, the natural state—since it is just the recognition of what we already are. Does it seem reasonable to believe that we can attain the effortless state through expending lots of effort? If we are already the One Consciousness that we are seeking, as many sages have asserted, then how hard should it be?

Jed McKenna asks, "How is it that so few are able to find the one thing that can never be lost?"

What if you are already unavoidably, inherently, eternally Here, and what if nothing can ever happen unless it happens Now? Then what would the point be of trying hard to keep remembering that inalterable fact?

I suggest contemplating the truth of this simple fact and move on to more significant questions.

Wouldn't it make more sense to recognize the ever-present nature of Here and Now and not impose a layer of effortful remembering on top of it? If it's always Here and Now, where and when would you look for it anyway? Any search for the present moment would be just a grand, self-delusional game of Hide-and-Seek where I pretend that Here and Now is somehow hidden, and I go running off in a desperate search to find it. Like a fish looking for water.

In such a galactic game of Hide-and-Seek with so many places to hide and so many things to seek, what outward search could ever hope to be successful? Perhaps only if I seek so hard and for so long that all hopes and dreams are completely shattered and I get so utterly exhausted playing the game that I just can't be enticed into seeking for one more round and I collapse in utter defeat, might there a chance to notice what remains after all is lost. This is called the Path of Effort. If you happen to find yourself on this path, my advice is to try harder. Spare no effort! It won't get you there, but you'll exhaust yourself sooner. And remember, you are not absolutely exhausted if you still have the thought, "I am really exhausted. Therefore, I must be getting close to awakening." If you are still harboring a strategy, you are not yet thoroughly played out. Try harder! More! Better! Higher!

The Path of Effort is a valid path and has worked for some, but like they say here in Tennessee, "It's a tough row to hoe." Thankfully, there is another possibility.

The preferable alternative (if you have a

choice) is to notice that it is utterly impossible to be anywhere other than Here or to experience anything at any time other than Now.

For example, you might be daydreaming about being on a beach in Tahiti watching tanned, almost-naked bodies frolicking in the transparent tropical waters while drinking an exotic fruit drink with a little umbrella in it. But where is that daydream actually taking place? Between your two ears, right? And what is noticing those thoughts passing through your MBU? Only consciousness can be conscious of those thoughts. If you were not conscious, you would not be aware of the daydream in the first place. As Henry David Thoreau said, "Only that day dawns to which we are awake." If you were unconscious, you couldn't even make the statement, "I am not conscious of my daydream." Therefore, if you are imagining the beach, those thought forms are happening in your Mind Body Unit (MBU) and are registered by consciousness. In other words, whatever you can imagine can only take place right where you are, i.e., Here.

Perhaps, one could argue that "Here" refers to abiding consciousness itself. However, consciousness is not spatially limited, so Here in that context would imply some large static state of consciousness. Why put consciousness in a noun box called Here? Why not let it expand or contract as it will? A swinging pendulum is in dynamic balance. Should we insist that the pendulum swing only to the left? If consciousness remains caught in a contracted, self-absorbed state, disharmony will result—the current condition of the world provides ample proof of that. However, the perpetually expanded, ethereal, objectless consciousness, if achievable, is also dysfunctional in this world. If objectless consciousness were the ultimate goal, what would be the point of all of this Creation? Full adult maturity is the recognition of our true being as consciousness, which functions through, and as, this MBU while at the same time being fully engaged in this Creation. God seems to be OK with consciousness flowing naturally between being narrowly attentive sometimes and resting in objectless awareness at other times. It just seems to be how Life is, and as I have come to realize after more than a few decades of exploring alternatives, it's unfruitful (and often painful) to argue with Life.

The consciousness that I'm speaking of is not some special, difficult-to-access, altered, elevated, spiritual consciousness. I'm talking about that common, plain vanilla, everyday, ordinary, run-of-the-mill awareness that is aware of your daydreams, your anger, your happiness, this next word, and everything else. In fact, it is fully functional in you (and everyone else) right this very moment.

So where is this consciousness located? Is there a you that is separate from this consciousness? Or is it more true to say that you exist and this consciousness is also always there—whether or not you are daydreaming and whether or not consciousness is in the foreground or the background? If there is a sense that you exist and consciousness also exists, are these really two things?

If you think so, then where are *you*—the real *you* not your MBU—located and where is consciousness located? Are there really two locations? Is there even one location? Or is consciousness present everywhere you look for it? Can you exist without consciousness? Can consciousness exist without you? Can you find any separation between the two?

If every thought or experience can be experienced only by consciousness, and if you and consciousness are inseparable, then every experience happens right where you always are: right here in ever-present consciousness. No effort required. You don't have to remember to be Here—you can never be anywhere else. Just notice the fact of it and relax. You are already home. You were never in Tahiti. The daydream about Tahiti is happening within the consciousness that you are.

Even if you do get on a plane and physically travel to Tahiti, the sunsets and the tropical breezes and the mai tai cocktails (and the silted lagoons) will all still be happening within the consciousness that you are.

Thinking that you are not already Here is just another thought in the mind. Consciousness will notice that thought also. Similarly, thinking that you were lost in some time other than Now can happen only in the mind. If we define ourselves by the thoughts passing through our minds (rather than as consciousness itself), then that same thinking mechanism can convince us of the necessity to try to be more present. However, if we recognize our True Nature as being consciousness itself, we are always Here and it is always Now, and, indeed, those terms cease to mean anything.

From the sun's perspective, the sun is always shining. From an earthling's viewpoint, sometimes it is shining and sometimes it isn't. Which is more fundamentally true?

If you are identified with what is happening in your mind, then sometimes it will be a clear day and sometimes it will be cloudy. When it's a cloudy day, you might conclude that you are unworthy of the sun. Ah, the mind is so clever that it can convince us of the impossible!

One of the problems with the directive to be more present is that most people aren't enjoying the Here in which they find themselves when they get up every morning, and they're trying in every way imaginable to get to a more pleasurable Here. (I guess logically that would be the imaginary There.) There are many popular avenues you can take to try to escape from the "ordinary" Here: alcohol, drugs, sex, movies, sports, politics, entertainment, personal drama, etc. There's nothing inherently wrong with any of these activities. They can all help us to forget about ourselves—however briefly. These pleasures hold the promise of transporting us to a more desirable state far removed from our recurring experience of "ordinary" life. Of course, these diversions all have their downsides, and as most of us have hopefully realized, none of them manage to keep the darkness or boredom at bay for long. In the words of 17th Century French Philosopher Blaise

Pascal, "Distraction is the only thing that consoles us for our miseries and yet it is itself the greatest of our miseries."

However, even while these efforts at self-distraction are pursued, our consciousness is still conscious of the experiences as they are happening. There's just no avoiding it, although we make every attempt—like a dog trying to run away from its own shadow. At least when a dog does it, it's funny.

Have you ever noticed that the whole world is happening within the consciousness that you are? I mean that literally. It's not a philosophical statement. It's a physiological fact that's beyond dispute. We think that the world exists outside us. We say, "I see a tree. The tree is over there." We recognize the form. It's similar to apple trees that we've seen before, so we know it might have apples on it. However, what is actually happening? Certain frequencies of light are being reflected off the tree. We see only those frequencies (colors) that our eyes have evolved to recognize—a miniscule fraction of the whole electromagnetic spectrum. The retinas of our eyes register the light wave pattern as electrochemical impulses which are conveyed deeper into the brain. The brain compares these impulses with impulses of similar patterns that it has encountered before and assigns meaning to them. An image of an apple tree is reconstituted in the brain and that image/pattern is witnessed by consciousness. We summarize that process by the words, "I see a tree." But the reality of the tree outside of ourselves is never encountered. It's the same process (using a different sense organ) if you walk over and hug the tree.

In addition, there might be personal conditioning associated with apple trees. For example, if you fell out of one when you were young, you will have a different current experience of this electrochemical stimulation than someone who has fond romantic memories of reclining with a loved one on a warm spring day under an apple tree in blossom. We see the world through the colored lenses of our conditioning.

When The brain reassembles this conditioned input into a visual image in the mind, and we say, "We see an apple tree." No, not true. We don't ever experience the tree directly! Our brains are just recognizing a pattern of electrical impulses from the optic nerve filtered through our past conditioning.

When we say we "see" the tree, we are simply conscious of the reconstituted image as it appears in our brain. It's similar to talking with someone on the telephone. We don't hear their actual voice; we hear electronically reconstituted vibrations that are a facsimile of their voice. We (unconsciously) conclude that it's close enough to reality to allow us to pretend that it is the other person's actual voice that we're listening to.

The final step where we register the image of the tree (or the voice on the phone) happens only within consciousness. It is consciousness that notices the image that is reconstructed within the brain. If there is no consciousness, then there is no image and no tree. You are that consciousness.

The whole world appears within that which you are.

Your Mind Body Unit (MBU) is the biological instrument that consciousness utilizes to experience the world. Apparently, even God needs instruments to witness Her own Creation! God needs your eyes to witness Her Creation. Meanwhile, you are looking everywhere for God! How diabolically funny is that?

Smell, touch, taste, thought, and bodily sensations (including emotions) operate the same way—like data input feeds. These inputs and your MBUs responses to them are projected onto the screen of consciousness.

It feels like the world is out there, but in fact it is all being experienced within the sensing mechanism of your MBU. So your entire experience of the world (as registered in your MBU) happens within consciousness. Every experience happens within your field of consciousness. So every experience is experienced by consciousness as occurring Here because it is the only place where it can ever occur.

And yet we can drive a car, cook a meal, play Hop Scotch, and hit a moving Ping Pong ball. How cool is that?! (Caution: Don't try to do these activities all at once. Nature still has rules.)

OK, so Here is unavoidable, but what about Now? We project linearity from an imaginary remembered past to an imaginary projected future, and in the middle there is this miniscule blip in that linear movement that we call Now.

Jed McKenna points out, "There is no now, there is only the intersection of past and future, both of which possess the curious charm of not existing."

What's really happening is just an ever-changing series of events.

The physicist John Wheeler once humorously said, "Time is what keeps everything from happening all at once." But time doesn't actually exist. It's just a convenient way for us to keep track of everything. Time is a conceptual convenience made up by mortal men, and it's arbitrary. It's a way to measure how quickly things are changing in appearance. I'm young; now I'm old. I'm pleasantly intoxicated; now I'm hungover. Life is always changing. Buddha told us 2,500 years ago that life is impermanent. No doubt! However, to measure those changes by how many times the Earth goes around the sun between when I wore nappies and when I grew a beard, or how many times I brush my teeth when the Earth spins around once on its own axis is just a man-made (Earth-centric) fabrication. There's nothing absolute about it.

The actuality is that it's always the present moment. It's not even a noun like a snapshot of the moment Now. It's more like a verb with an ever-changing scenery set that you're always witness to. This Now is ever-present, inescapable, dynamic, and alive. Trying to be in the Now utterly misses the beautiful fluidity of the impermanence of Life.

So I guess my mother was right after all when

she said, as she often did, "There's no time like the present," although in retrospect I believe she was probably talking less about the nature of reality and more about chores that I hadn't yet done. (Or maybe she wasn't. I guess I'm not sure)

Ram Dass sent us down a path of effort to try to be more present, when Here and Now are unavoidable, ever-present facets of Life. In fairness to Ram Dass, I believe he was pointing beyond the obvious facts of Here and Now to the consciousness within which apparent space and time exist. I also believe that he knew, or now knows, the effort to be Here and Now is a teaching tool, as all spiritual statements are (at best!), and he was trying to get us to notice how much energy we spend rehashing past events or contemplating future possibilities, neither of which actually exist.

Rather than spinning your wheels by trying to get somewhere more spiritual, simply recognize the wonder that consciousness is. It will free you to explore two critical questions:

Question #1: Is consciousness a biological

function of your brain cells, or is your bodymind a manifestation within consciousness?

Question #2: In your own direct experience, without resorting to thought or concepts, are *you* in any way separate from (or other than) consciousness?

These are not razor-thin philosophical distinctions—they are the difference between imprisonment and freedom. Allow yourself to ponder. Open yourself to the possibility that *you* may not be what you have always thought you were. Explore the ever-present reality of consciousness. Only your direct experience counts. Don't worry about getting it wrong the first hundred times you look. Truth is never absent, and you are never far away.

The worst-case scenario is that you imagine that you are separate and isolated from God. However, it isn't actually possible to be separate from the One Existence. There is not an alternate Universe somewhere. If and when we ever experience the umpty-umpth dimension that some physicists postulate, it too will be experienced within consciousness.

There is only one thing happening. So there's no way you can be separate from it.

Notice that the gift has already been given.

Take a seat at the table.

Rejoice in this m...o...m...e...n...t!

Forever and ever-changing. Life without end.

# Myth #8

"It Takes Lifetimes to Undo All My Bad Karma"

The concept of karma is one of those things that we imported from Asia a few decades ago and has settled comfortably into our Western psyche. The idea conforms to what we were told early in our school careers, which was that everything went on our "permanent record." Karma reportedly tracks you from lifetime to lifetime. And Butch Cassidy thought he had it tough! The theory is that there is good karma and there is bad karma, and the mere fact that we were born into this life means that we had some negative karma to work through because otherwise we'd be freed from rebirth. Of course, this begs the question of why we were ever born into our first lifetime. Wait a minute. This starts sounding a lot like the concept of original sin—that we are somehow defective from the get go, but we can't quite recall why. In any event, we've come to accept this negative bias. We assume that there's something inherently wrong with us, and our job in this life is to make amends.

Santayana [the Spanish philosopher] said: "Those who do not learn from history are doomed to repeat it." Byron Katie has a similar saying: "Karma is just an unexplored belief." In other words, whatever we believe, we get to experience over and over again until we take a really close and objective look at the assumption(s) underlying our belief. Our beliefs color our reality. And our assumptions are never absolutely true. We start with a faulty foundation and build a lifetime of beliefs on top of it. Our job this lifetime is to see through our beliefs and free ourselves to experience what is actually happening.

So, is it true that it takes lifetimes to undo

past karma? How did we come to believe this? We weren't born with this belief hard-wired into our MBUs. Somewhere we read it or heard someone say it, and we believed it. But do we really, absolutely, 100 percent, without-a-doubt know it to be true in our own experience?

First of all, do you even know for sure if this whole reincarnation thing is true? Even if you've remembered past lives, didn't you experience those memories while living *this* life? So, besides your wish for it to be so, how do you know (for sure) that those memories were not just vivid dreams? Or maybe all the remembered lifetimes including this current one are happening concurrently, and it just depends which eyes you're looking through. I'm not saying that reincarnation is not real; I am saying if you don't know then it's OK not to know. It's OK to hold it as an open question. Awakening is not about adopting the proper set of dogmas; it's about finding that which cannot be lost. The path is through not-knowing. Beliefs are obstacles. It seems to me that this current lifetime provides us with ample mental and experiential fodder for our frail little bodyminds to sort through.

As the Buddha said, "If you want to know what you did in your past life, observe your current condition. If you want to know what your future condition will be, observe your present actions."

Meister Eckhart, 14th century Christian mystic advised, "In this birth you will discover all blessing. But neglect this birth and you neglect all blessing. Tend only to this birth in you and you will find there all goodness and consolation, all delight, all being and all truth."

So now that we can perhaps hold our ideas about karma and reincarnation a little more lightly, maybe I dare ask if you know for certain that bad karma can be undone by doing good deeds? And even if that were true, how do you know with certainty what actions you should take to produce "good" karma? Have your actions in this lifetime always produced the beneficent results you intended? Or is it more of a mixed bag?

In looking back at our lives, if we're honest with ourselves, we have all done or said things that have hurt other people. We've all been petty sometimes, perhaps been downright mean on occasion (or more often than that), or have been somewhat less than forthright in some of our dealings with others. And then, of course, there are the biggies such as greed, anger, hatred, jealousy, and righteousness—perhaps not excessively so if we compare ourselves to others—but chances are that we're probably not at the extreme saintly end of the spectrum either. So can we say—even for this lifetime—that we're way ahead on the good karma side of the ledger? Or is it more like 90/10? How about 80/20?

So what are the chances of staying on the straight and narrow for the next umpteen lifetimes? In this current lifetime we've heard about karma and can maybe do something about it, but what guarantee do we have that we will even hear about it in our next lifetime? Whoops, maybe our multi-lifetime project is at risk already!

And then there is the problem of not always knowing the right action to take. Good intentions often have unintended consequences. Maybe we've known someone who was down and out, so we loaned them some money to get a new start and they used it to go out and buy drugs. (I've done that—loaned the money, that is.) Maybe we married someone we thought we loved, and it turned into suffering for both of us. Maybe we held our children to such high standards that they revolted and adopted self-destructive behavior. It's difficult enough to know what choices will turn out positively for us; it's at least as difficult to know what's best for others.

Good intentions can sometimes lead to bad outcomes. Good intentions executed on a grand scale can have catastrophic consequences. Those who implemented the Spanish Inquisition believed that the torture and killing of non-believers was in service to their Catholic God. Some people decide to bomb crowded marketplaces in order to please Allah. There are countless other tragic examples. Perhaps throughout all history, more people have been killed in the pursuit of "lofty" intentions than from all the epidemics, starvation, drugs, gang violence, and murders combined. You or I would never get caught up in any such mass madness—or so we imagine. It's one thing to believe that my idea of God is the correct one, and anyone who doesn't share my beliefs is wrong. It's quite another thing to fly planes into buildings—or maybe the difference is only a question of degree.

Now, to be clear, I think it's fine to want to help your neighbor or volunteer in the community or donate to a worthy cause or try to alleviate suffering in some direct, hands-on way or even to serve when called upon. Personally, I would much rather live in a world where people are at least trying to be kind and considerate and loving to one another. However, if we are acting in a way that we believe is "good" in order to gain favor in the afterlife, or in order to feel, "Oh, what a wonderful person am I," or in order to undo "bad" karma so that we can advance spiritually, then we are engaged in horse trading. We are giving something to get something, hopefully something of equal or greater value! We're trading good deeds for future rewards. And we imagine that we're on a path to selflessness!

Doing "good deeds" can be tricky. I once knew a woman—the mother of a friend of mine—who went to church every day of her life, literally. Her cousin lived the fast life of a "showgirl" in Las Vegas for many years until that life no longer paid the bills. My friend's mother then took her in and cared for her. On the surface, the facts make the mother seem noble. However, what I witnessed as a young man was a business deal: The mother gained a sense of righteousness, and the former showgirl adopted an identity of shame, guilt, and dependence. Like a thief and a home-alarm salesperson, an arsonist and a fireman, or a sinner and a priest, it was a less-than-healthy, codependent relationship.

I know that I went on at some length about

the potentially slippery slope of helping others, but it seems that we all believe that we know what is good, especially when the term is used in the phrase "good for others." I'm just trying to introduce a little doubt into that certainty.

So if your plan is to devote this lifetime—and maybe many subsequent lifetimes—to doing good deeds to undo bad karma, before we start out on that arduous journey, shouldn't we at least ask the question, "Do I know that what I am doing is truly good for all involved?" Not an easy question. And if I can answer that question in the affirmative, "Do I know that there is really a scorecard somewhere and a scorekeeper noting the entries?" It feels conceivable, perhaps fueled by our collective fear of being judged by others, but do you know for sure? Remember, you're betting your life energy on the answer.

The danger of this particular myth is that it is fear-based. Also, we are focused on the future, and life is happening now. If we believe that we will become eligible for awakening only after years and years of service to others, we will miss the ever-present opportunity to awaken right now in this lifetime.

And I guarantee that if you awaken now, you will be much more likely to be of genuine service to others during your remaining years. It's like they tell you on the airplane before you take off: put your own oxygen mask on first, then assist your child. The first time I heard that announcement, it sounded anti-child, but then I realized that if you're unconscious, you won't be of much assistance to anybody.

However, the real fallacy to this myth about needing many lifetimes to undo all your bad karma is that maybe you have *already* invested the requisite number of lifetimes doing good deeds, and in fact, THIS life is the life you are due to awaken and NOW is the moment!

Don't procrastinate! We all tend to leave things until the last minute, whether it's homework, paying taxes, or forgiving a grievance. Deadlines help us focus our attention. In this life, we've been given a wonderful deadline. It's called death. Be grateful. Without the prospect of death to grab our attention, we probably wouldn't ever get around to doing anything of real value.

To paraphrase the Buddha, you have the amazing good fortune to be alive, even more good fortune to have been born in human form, fortunate to have heard about awakening. And fortunate to live in an age where true teachers are available for free on the Internet or at your local bookstore for less than the price of a movie ticket. And, if you are reading this, you probably have a full belly and a warm bed to sleep in safety tonight. Of all possible births, you are blessed indeed!

Be grateful for this opportunity to awaken. Don't allow yourself to be convinced that you will find a better opportunity in some future life. If you tell yourself, "Oh well, I'll deal with this awakening thing next lifetime if it doesn't happen this lifetime," it takes the pressure off. It's like hitting the snooze button on a Monday morning. Use the deadline you've been given to focus your attention.

No matter what your current economic, employment, health, relational, or legal circumstances, you are very, very fortunate. Be grateful. It has all been a setup to get you here—right to the brink.

There is no better time than right now to fall into awakening.

Use *this* life to find out who (or what) *you* really are—it's the ultimate journey.

Grant karma its due, but make yourself available to the possibility of awakening without further ado.

# Myth #7

"I Have to Purify Myself First"

We humans just assume that we are flawed: we do things we know we shouldn't do; we say things we know we shouldn't say; we buy things we know won't make us happy—at least not for very long; we enter into relationships we know we shouldn't; we believe things that aren't true. And as long as we believe that we are each limited to this separate little Mind Body Unit (MBU), we naturally conclude that we are flawed. We judge ourselves guilty, convict ourselves for our weaknesses, and sentence ourselves to a lifetime of digging our way out of a hole that we don't know how we got into. But then we hear about the possibility of parole, and imagine a life beyond the confines of the prison walls at some long distant date.

In the meantime, consciousness is sitting back in the visitor's gallery witnessing this whole courtroom drama with a curious amused detachment.

"So how," we ask, "do I earn the right to be considered for parole? What do I have to do?" We are advised by other prisoners to clean up our act to make ourselves more eligible. "That seems like reasonable advice," we think. "But what exactly should I do?"

"Should I become a vegetarian, or maybe even a vegan? Or maybe I'll skip to the front of the enlightenment line if I eat only fruit. Should I give up that glass of wine that seems to make French people healthy? Do I need to trade in my grande caramel mocha for a cup of green tea? Do I need to lose weight to look more yogic? Do sexual pleasures really drain my vital energies as claimed by the deranged General in *Dr. Strangelove?* Do I need to get the right meditation cushion, go live in a cave, burn more incense, have an altar in my bedroom, analyze my dreams, keep a diary, read more books, shave my head, give away my leather shoes, go to India, give up smoking, put more affirmations on my bathroom mirror, start referring to myself in the third person, change my 'ism,' believe in God, forgive my parents (or maybe I need to renounce my family), go to a psychologist to work things out with my partner, or should I just leave my partner to go on my quest?" And those are the easy questions. Then, of course, there are the significantly more difficult ones like becoming more humble, being unselfish, not getting angry, telling the truth, being responsible, giving up pride—I could go on but maybe you already have your own "to do" list.

There are seemingly so many aspects to improve and so much of our conditioned selves to put right. We could spend a lifetime just trying to figure out what we should be doing and at least several more to implement all our desired changes.

My father recently died at age ninety-four. He was a capable man and yet, when he died, he still had a file drawer (yes, literally a file drawer) filled with lists of how he needed to improve himself. On one hand, you might say, "How admirable that a person that old still had the desire to improve." On the other hand, let his life serve as a caution that even ninety-four years may not be anywhere near enough time to work through all one's perceived shortcomings.

If we insist that all of these self-assessed inadequacies have to be resolved before we can realize our true nature, then we will have succeeded in postponing our awakening indefinitely. We will have constructed a mental barricade just this side of heaven, and we will imagine that we're making progress as we try to dissemble it piece by piece.

Steven Harrison suggests that, "We can continue our quest for improvement or not. We can search for happiness, enlightenment, security or identity or not. The search is not wrong; it is unrelated to the actual world." "Personal improvement is like sitting in a movie theater, arguing with the villain projected on the screen, and feeling that at least we have tried to make things better."

One difficulty with this purify-yourself-first approach is that these habits are habitual for good reason. Somewhere along the way, usually in our early years, we learned behaviors that we believed we needed just to get by. As kids, we were genuinely confused by the adults who were seemingly running the show, so we adopted conditioned responses that we (unconsciously) believed would be in our best interest. These behaviors were often intended to protect our frail little selves or, at least, to minimize our discomfort or pain.

Our biological ancestors lived in a world where they were confronted with the very real possibility of being chased by saber-toothed tigers. Our brains have not evolved all that much in the last few hundred generations, but our modern tigers have gotten much stealthier.

We have a logical, reasonable, but often confused, forebrain, and we have a deeper more primitive but more powerful reptilian brain that houses our survival instinct. Our logical brain thinks that our primitive brain should be subordinate and submissive to our forebrain's logic. The primitive brain says "Huh?" and offers up a different agenda. When we know it's sensible to put away the bag of chocolate chip cookies, our primitive brain says, "No, I *need* those cookies to keep the loneliness (boredom, depression, darkness, whatever) at bay." One part of us knows what we *should* do, and another part knows what we *need* to do to survive. Maybe we need those cookies only to survive an otherwise boring evening, or to get us through the next TV commercial, but it is still perceived by the primitive brain as essential for our self-preservation. There is internal conflict. The tiger is lurking just there in the shadows. Guess who generally wins the fight.

Maybe your logical brain can win Round #1 and you put down the cookie. Ten minutes later the primitive brain again needs to be reassured. Maybe your logical brain also wins Round #2. But can your rational mind go all fifteen rounds? Your primitive brain has to win only one round, you eat the cookie, and the behavior is reinforced. It hardly seems fair! The primitive mind is only temporarily satiated. Habits are formed beyond the easy reach of our rational mind. Our rational mind wants to break the habit, but that's not where the conditioning resides. We remain conflicted. And thoroughly conditioned.

Many of the things that we do are done out of conditioning, such as walking, talking, reading, typing, and brushing our teeth. When we first did these things as young children, they required our full attention. Now, we can do them mindlessly. We have conditioned our MBUs to do these things without thought. If you doubt the extent of your conditioning, try brushing your teeth with your other hand!

Not all conditioning is bad. Personally, I enjoy reading, walking and driving a car, but the conditioning that does cause us (and others) problems is our unconscious emotional reactions.

Generally, these dysfunctional emotional behaviors are strategies that were unconsciously adopted in our early years. Our unruly primitive brain has concluded that these strategies, sometimes even the self-destructive ones, are in our own best self-interest. So what chance do we really have to deny ourselves these strategies that we *know* sub-consciously are there to protect us? Usually not much of a chance. So we remain immersed in our own conditioning, even when we are aware of it—even when we try for years to change it.

One of the widely experienced, but not generally known, ways in which the world works is that the harder you try to change a habit, the more you empower it. It's like an escalating Cold War inside your head. Your rational mind tries harder to change, and your primitive mind digs in its heels to protect itself. The conflict amps up, but fear always trumps logic, and the habit remains firmly in place.

Adyashanti advises, "What you run away from owns you. You are the dog on a leash. The most you can do is to tug against the leash."

Just ask any struggling addict. The hopeless drunk knows that what he is doing is self-destructive, but he continues the behavior because there is also a deeper psychological (and physiological) conditioning that says that the alcohol is necessary just to get through another day. There is internal conflict. The primitive brain needs to be comforted. The rational brain cannot be relied upon to win all fifteen rounds, every day, against such a powerful, stubborn, and elusive adversary.

With help and effort and attention and maybe with a support group if necessary, perhaps we can give up a destructive habit or two. But then there are still so many other things to try to purify. And if we try too hard to be too perfect, we make ourselves—and everyone else around us—grumpy (or worse!), and then that becomes one more thing that we have to work on.

The concept of purifying ourselves before we

can enter the preliminary qualifying round for awakening, although noble in intent, is just too much to expect from our thoroughly conditioned, frail little MBUs.

Fortunately though, the belief that you need to purify yourself in order to awaken is simply not true. It's nothing more than a myth! I know that's not what you'd expect, but purity is not a prerequisite for awakening.

There are no prerequisites for waking up. Drunk or teetotaler. Neat or sloppy. Successful or unemployed. Married or single. Worthy or not. Confused or clear-headed. Happy or depressed. Together or a basket case. It simply doesn't matter. Any belief otherwise just gets in the way. Surprised? I was too.

Take some time to bask in the possibility that you don't have to implement a personal twelve-step program to purify all your bad habits before Grace will glance your way.

Awakening is like a "special introductory offer"—a gift. Grace. Purity is not a prerequisite.

However, there is the matter of life *after* awakening. I know the commonly accepted belief is that you get to live happily ever after, which is true in the sense that there is a deep contentment that remains if the awakening "sticks." However, although it is not necessary to purify all your habits, addictions, and beliefs *before* awakening, you will have to face your shadow side eventually—if not before then after awakening. The light of awareness is a jealous lover; it will seek out any remaining areas of darkness. It may happen over time, but you will have to deal with those shadow areas sooner or later.

Now, I know that Nisargadatta smoked like a chimney and Jesus enjoyed a glass or possibly two of vino with his supper, but what I am talking about is the emotionally charged conditioning that can cause you to suffer—even after awakening. (When asked about his smoking, Nisargadatta simply said, "It's just a habit." It might not have been good for his health, but it wasn't causing him any emotional distress.)

Some, perhaps many, thoroughly conditioned, emotionally charged habits, points of stuckness, etc., will be released at the moment of awakening itself. However, it is very unlikely that all of them will be discharged so effortlessly. The rest of them will remain to be seen through after awakening. I know this isn't what they tell you in the spiritual marketing material, and admittedly there are no rules, so perhaps you will be the one person in ten thousand that wakes up to a life of perpetual everlasting bliss with all of your self-limiting conditioning fading effortlessly into permanent oblivion. I'm not saying that it won't happen that way for you; I suppose it could, but don't count on it.

So you might ask, "If I have to deal with these issues eventually anyway, where's the good news?" Well, the good news is that it's vastly easier to deal with these deeply conditioned behaviors after awakening.

It is consciousness that wakes up to itself. There is a realization (maybe not initially, but as the awakening matures) that consciousness is not personal. At some point after awakening (if awakeness is allowed full reign), a shift of identity occurs. It is a shift from knowing that you are fundamentally consciousness to actually living from that consciousness. These two perspectives may sound similar, but experientially, they are worlds apart.

The paradigm before we awaken is that we are all separate little individuals walking around in a great big universe, and that each of us has a subordinate attribute of our mind that we refer to as *our* consciousness. (One day, surely scientists will find it in there somewhere!) With awakening, consciousness is recognized as primary and that the entire Universe, including this MBU that we claim as ours, occurs within that consciousness. It may take some time after awakening before this permanent change of identity solidifies and the recognition occurs that only One Consciousness exists. It seems odd that the understanding can occur in a flash and yet the shift may take place only gradually, but that is how it played out for me. The shift was apparent only in hindsight.

As you can imagine, it's far easier to deal with personal issues from the vantage point of impersonal awareness than it is from the standpoint of it being my problem. For example, it's far easier for you to know how your parents, or partner, or boss should change than it is to change yourself. Why is that? Because you are not so invested in their unique brand of conditioning. This less personal perspective begins to emerge after awakening. You still have to see through the illusion, but you are not so heavily invested. Therefore, you can observe your habits more objectively. It feels more like a sociological study and less like self-surgery. Who knows? Over time, you may even learn to enjoy the undoing process! John Prendergast characterizes this compassionate investigation as being like an "affectionate anthropologist."

Despite the connotations of the word "impersonal," impersonal consciousness does not distance you from Life; rather it is a freedom that allows you to fully engage in Life on Life's terms without fear.

The vantage point makes all the difference. Before awakening, there is internal division—one thought demands change, while another, deeper belief holds on for dear life. After awakening, you will have learned that the journey onward is one of letting go simply because holding on is just too painful. The need to defend your emotionally charged positions is seen as pointless and the source of suffering. Clarity erodes conditioning.

You don't have to try to undo anything. Your only job is to be willing to allow dysfunctional conditioning to arise, see and feel it clearly, as it is without judgment. The light of awareness does the unwinding in a most mysterious way. This process can proceed before awakening and it will (more insistently) proceed after awakening.

Take comfort in the news that purity is not required before waking up. But please know that I am not saying that it's therefore OK to be a jerk and act out all your stuff. Be open to the possibility of awakening now.

And be compassionate. Compassion is not just something to offer others, although that is certainly a worthy practice in itself. Compassion is also something you can offer yourself. You got conditioned in childhood. Big deal! So did everyone else. Maybe yours was heavier than most others. It's still OK to stop playing the victim and move on. It was just the unique hand that you were dealt. Who knows? Maybe you even chose your particular situation prior to taking this birth in order to have exactly the experience that you are now having. Imagine that! Maybe from the perspective of pure consciousness before adopting your particular MBU it even seemed like a good idea in order to have the opportunity to see through a certain blockage or to satisfy some karmic debt. Again, who knows? However, if we allow that possibility, it softens the relationship with our own (perhaps challenging) story. In any case, the *cause* of your childhood (or more recent) trauma is in the past and is not now occurring in this moment. Learn from it and find the capacity to be grateful for it—after all, it helped to get you here where you are willing to contemplate the essential nature of your existence. And let it go. Generally, the next to last people we are willing to forgive are those who have "harmed" us. The last person we are willing to forgive is usually ourselves. It's OK to offer compassion to ourselves too. After all, we're only human.

In the original Greek (the language of the first Biblical texts), the word "sin" was an archery term that meant "to miss the mark." Well, that takes a lot of the forcefulness out of the word "sin," doesn't it? You missed the mark. You acted unskillfully. You now have an opportunity to learn from the experience and behave more skillfully the next time. Did you notice that I am fond of the word "skillful" in this context? It's a word that I am borrowing from Fred Davis. I like it because viewing one's behavior as more or less skillful certainly gives life a different feel than judging everything in a dualistic manner as good or bad, right or wrong, saintly or sinful.

To sum up:

Don't do so much planning that you never get on the plane. No one ever got to Disneyland by just reading travel brochures.

It's fine to make the effort to round off a few of our rough edges. Just don't conclude that we have to be perfect (or even better than average) in order to wake up.

Start fishing with the bait you already have!

Or as Jesus said, "Seek ye first the Kingdom of God." He didn't say, "Clean up your act first, then let's talk."

And, by the way, there is no gate except the one you yourself imagine into existence.

# Myth #6

"I Must Transcend All Thought"

In every good drama, there needs to be an antagonist, a.k.a. "the bad guy." In the spiritual awakening drama, our thinking mind is often assigned this role. Some teachers have said that thinking and spirituality are inversely related; that is, the less you think, the more spiritual you are. By logical extrapolation then, we should envy those in a coma. But isn't this just backwards? To say, "If we think less, we will wake up" is different than saying, "If we wake up to the realization that I am consciousness prior to content, random thought will tend to become less and less interesting to me and will likely recede over time." You be the judge. Which resonates as being more true?

When you tell yourself that you must be free of all thought in order to awaken, is this not itself just another thought? And do you actually know if it's true? Or is it just something someone asserted and you thought it sounded like a worthy goal (perhaps because it sounded so ridiculously difficult).

What is your own experience of the phenomena of thinking? You have, after all, had a lifetime in the company of your own mind. Thinking seems to be happening virtually all the time, does it not? So, by now, you are uniquely positioned to answer this question: Do you have control over your thoughts? Can you turn your thoughts on and off on command, or do thoughts just happen and you watch the parade whether you want to or not? Even if you have the thought, "Now, I want to start to think about spaghetti," where did that thought come from? Did you decide to think it, and if so, where did the thought to think it come from?

Etc., etc. It is impossible to argue that you control your thoughts without basing your position on an endless regression of conceptual thought with no point of origin. Would it not be more accurate to say that thoughts just happen? When they happen, you are happy to take credit for the ones you like and are eager to disown the ones you don't.

Consider that the mind is just another organ in the body. The heart pumps blood. The kidneys filter out waste products. The spleen does whatever the heck it does, and the mind thinks thoughts. It's just what the organ called the mind does. Who am I to tell it that it shouldn't? (I realize that the mind does other things too, but those other things don't cause emotional contraction. Only thoughts can do that.)

If we look closely at the thoughts in our mind, we can soon notice that thoughts have a lifespan. They arise, hang around for a while, and then recede back into the silence from whence they arose. They pass like shooting stars through our minds. OK, you're right; only the pleasant thoughts are like shooting stars—the unpleasant ones are more like ox carts that can take days (or perhaps years) to pass from view.

A useful inquiry is whether they are even *your* thoughts. Are they really unique to you? Or is it more accurate to say that some are Mom's, some are Dad's, some are from the TV, and some came from your teachers, or a coach, or a friend, or from the last book you read, etc. If you had been born into another culture, another family, or had different friends, would you still have the same thoughts? Perhaps you came into this life with some emotional bleed-through from a prior life. Perhaps some conditioned thoughts came from your mom or dad or spouse in a prior life, etc. And from where did they get their conditioned thoughts? When viewed objectively, it's difficult to find a thought that we can truly claim is ours.

It's like God hearing about original sin. His response is always, "Nope, I heard it before."

However, one thing is certain: the thoughts in our head go on and on and on and . . .

Perhaps it's time to sit yourself down and admit out loud, "My name is ____. I am an addict. I am addicted to thinking. I have no control over it. I don't know how I got into this fix. I've tried to stop, but I can't. I acknowledge my helplessness in this regard."

I am actually not joking. Try it. See if it doesn't feel true. It's OK to admit when something is true.

However, what if the critical issue is not the presence or absence of thought, but whether or not you *believe* the thoughts that you're thinking? Doesn't that feel different?

The only thoughts that have any emotional power over you are the ones that you believe. And you do have a choice. Just know that if you choose to believe any emotionally charged thought, you are choosing to anchor your identity in ego-land and your True Nature will be obscured for the duration. Not that your True Nature is absent in any way, but it is easily obscured by the power of your beliefs. (We humans are immensely powerful. We can obscure the Infinite by a single believed thought!)

If your favorite team is the Cowboys, it's not a problem. However, if you believe that anyone who roots for the Seahawks is demented and diminishes the consciousness of the planet... well, maybe it's time to do a little inquiry around that one.

Sound farfetched? Substitute the words "Republicans" and "Democrats" for the team names in the prior paragraph and check in to see if there's any emotional juice in it for you.

However, if thoughts are just passing through and you are neither fascinated nor repelled by them, are they of any real concern? Are not disregarded thoughts just background noise, like elevator music? Do you become less "spiritual" when you step into an elevator? (A: Only if you hold an opinion that they shouldn't let some second rate orchestra play "Hey Jude.")

If you are on a crowded subway with a carload of noisy passengers and a blaring boom-box (do they still make those anymore?), but you are there with your new lover, the sounds certainly vibrate your eardrums as they do others on the subway, but they have little importance to you. On the other hand, if you are in the same subway but now you are alone and tired and had a hard day at work and you have the belief that these people shouldn't be so noisy, and they should be more respectful of others, and they ought to outlaw boom boxes . . . it's the same subway, but an entirely different experience.

Sometimes, if you meditate or if you spend some quiet time having a cup of tea or if you wander out in Nature or if you get shocked by suddenly noticing a snake underfoot or if you are stunned silly by the punch line of a joke, the thought stream in your head might stop for a moment. If you have been trying to eliminate thinking as part of your spiritual practice, you might even be spared a commenting thought like, "Gee, I'm really getting good at this not-thinking thing." But let's be honest: Can you really claim credit when the thought stream temporarily ceases or take the blame when it arises again? I know that's what we do, but is it a valid conclusion? Isn't it more accurate to say when the thought stream temporarily stops that it does so spontaneously—without any doing on our part? We can notice it, but we can't control it. But noticing makes all the difference. Simple noticing—without trying to change anything—is the key. You notice when thoughts are there and you notice when they're not, without trying to manipulate the experience either way.

It seems as if the harder we try to make the thought stream stop, the noisier our mind gets. Why is that? It seems counter-intuitive. Our willpower usually works well in other areas of our life, so why doesn't it work when we try to control our thoughts? Well, because the only thing trying to stop thought is just another thought, and that particular thought is in conflict with the reality of a mind whose job it is to think. When we further energize our already-busy, thinking mind with an opposing thought, should we really be surprised if the result is more energized thinking?

The simple fact is that thought is occurring. And Reality is not responsive to what we think should be, or shouldn't be, happening. Have you noticed? We might like the thought or not, but regardless, it's what's happening.

We may not be able to change the thoughts in our head, but we can change our *relationship* with those thoughts.

When we attempt to control thought, we are trying to exert control in an arena where we have none. Instead of adding to the conflict, why not just acknowledge the lack of control and relax about it? When we relax about the content of our minds, the odd thing is that the noise tends to subside. It may take a little time to settle down, but if you quit shaking the jar, the mud will eventually settle out and clarity is given the chance to emerge. Like so many things in spirituality, it's counter-intuitive. If you've had the beast (your mind) on a short leash your whole life, it might run around crazily for a while when you first release it. That's natural. Dogs in the park do the same thing. But if you stop chasing them or running away from them, they will gradually settle down and act sane. So will your mind.

So why are we trying to stop the thought stream in the first place? Maybe we just want a little peace and quiet. Maybe we believe it is spiritually beneficial to be thought-free. But is that thought true? Sure, some thoughts can be annoying, but don't forget, some can be quite pleasurable. If we don't get hooked into identifying with either, there is no problem. There's no need to chase a thought stream just because it's a pleasant daydream, nor is it necessary to try to silence a thought stream that we aren't enjoying. Just see that neither is fundamentally true.

Imagine a fish in the river and a fisherman. (Sorry, but "fisherperson" just sounds too stilted.) The fisherman keeps trying different lures. He/she knows that certain lures have worked well in the past. If a fish believes the lure to be real, it will bite, get hooked, and suffer. However, if the fish is neither attracted by the false bait nor so upset by the splashy-splashy of the lure repeatedly thrown in the surrounding water that it attacks the lure out of spite, then there is no problem and eventually the fisherman (your mind) will tire of playing the game.

So, like the disinterested fish, even if thoughts are still present, who cares?

Whoa there, speed-reader! "Who cares?" is the essential question. *Who* is it that cares? Exactly?

Let's say that there is an event, and then there is a mental or an emotional response to that event. OK, but how do *you* take possession of either the event or your response to the event? Neither belong to *you*. The event happened and the response is the result of countless moments of prior conditioning. This is what sages mean when they say that we are all sleepwalking or that we are living a dream-like, robotic existence. You always have the choice of whether to "own" the event or not.

Let's say that your friend says something

mean to you. Perhaps fairly, perhaps not. That is the event. So far, no problem. So far, it's just your friend's opinion to which he/she is entitled. It's the next mental step, if faulty, that can create suffering. If you conclude that your friend spoke unfairly and he/she *shouldn't* have said that or that maybe your friend is right about you and you really are a terrible person, then, either way, you will suffer. Your friend is not causing you to suffer; you do that to yourself. There is the event and then there is your reaction to the event and then sometimes there is your generalization about your reaction to the event, which are second and third levels of abstraction from reality.

You don't need to stop thinking to gain peace, you just need to see through the falsity of your thoroughly conditioned, mental processes.

See deeply into the transitory, impersonal nature of thought, and it won't matter whether thinking is there or not. When you see that it doesn't matter, interest in the whole thinking/not thinking game tends to subside. And then over time, usually in hindsight, you realize that the mind has gotten quieter. And then, even when a conditioned thought runs through your mind, it is seen as inconsequential background noise.

And then, out of the blue when we occasionally forget to try to stop thinking, we are graced with a brief intermission. Ahhh! And then we want more. We ask, "How can I do that again?" Again we want something other than what is. And again we are energizing our mind.

Now, just to be clear, there are three kinds of thinking that are useful and non-problematic: functional thought, self-inquiry, and creative thought.

If you are at work, functional thought is often required—it's what people get paid to do. Functional thought has proven to be a driving force of our civilization. Functional thought solves problems and gets things done. It writes software, learns how to raise tomatoes, builds tall buildings, etc. Using functional thought as the valuable tool it is, when it is needed, is obviously not problematic.

We can also use thought to inquire into how we are "illusioning" ourselves. (I know that "illusioning" probably isn't a real verb, but it sure seems like it would be valuable to learn how to dis-illusion ourselves!) This type of objective self-inquiry can be very useful in seeing through the nature of thought itself. The image of using a thorn to pluck out an embedded thorn is often used to illustrate self-inquiry; that is, using words to get beyond words, using the mind to see the limits of thought, and using logic to approach the place where logic morphs into the paradoxical world of non-duality. Then, from this place of unknowing, ask a heart-felt question and let it marinate without trying to come up with a comfortable, conceptual answer. This is useful inquiry.

The third kind of non-problematic thought is creative thought, which is using the mind to "capture" creative impulses that originate beyond our MBUs, but that require a living, breathing MBU to bring such impulses into this world. Examples would be music composition, poetry, architecture, art, creative writing, and sometimes deep scientific insight.

Since we can probably agree that functional thought, objective self-inquiry, and creative thought are not the categories of thought that cause us grief, for the rest of this chapter, when we refer to thought, we will mean the other 95 percent—you know, those sticky thoughts that are just repetitive, silly, petty, juvenile, commenting, unloving, spiteful, wishful, regretful, justifying, misinformed, conditioned, inherited, adopted, unforgiving, desiring and so on. We all have our own patterns. Is this nonfunctional, nonproductive thought stream enjoyable? Does it improve life? Do you feel better when you engage in it? These kinds of conditioned, recurring thought patterns can imprison us for years (or even for our entire life) within the emotional states they energize. We tend to be our own prosecuting attorney, judge, and jury, and we are not generally in a very forgiving mood.

Unfortunately, trying to forcibly get rid of these dysfunctional thoughts simply doesn't work. We've all tried not to think about something that was bothering us, but does it ever work for long? Eventually, the repressed thought-stream returns and it usually does so with renewed vengeance exactly when our defenses are down—like when we wake up at 3:00 a.m.

Only when we clearly see that a conditioned thought is simply not true is the thought de-energized. When we can clearly see the falseness of a belief, the belief will drop away without effort. But, we have to make the effort to see through it in the first place. It's like touching an electric fence. People tell you not to do it, but maybe you do it anyway. You only have to do it once to know that it will only cause pain. Once you know that, you don't have to try to resist the temptation to touch the fence—there's just nothing in you that wants to do it. Seeing deeply through an unskillful behavior is like that, except some dysfunctional behaviors are part pleasure and part pain and can sometimes take (a lot) more than one touch to realize that the pleasure is not worth the pain it causes yourself or others.

And by "see through it," I don't mean analyze it. How many people do you know (perhaps know very well) who have spent half their adult lives going to see therapists and now can explain in excruciating detail how and why they are dysfunctional? They are still screwed up, but now they can spend hours describing it to you eloquently. Perhaps even enthusiastically! You could call this glibness "gallows humor light." One could organize Tupperware® style parties where people get together to share stories and commiserate happily about how screwed up they are. "You think that's bad, well my therapist told me that . . . ." Oh, I guess people do that already.

To "see through" a conditioned thought, I mean seeing its inherent falseness. For example, let's say you have the more-common-than-you-would-think thought: "I'm unworthy." You weren't born with that thought; you learned it along the way after you were taught words and concepts. Maybe someone you trusted told you that you wouldn't ever amount to anything and you believed it, or they laid out the criteria for worthiness and you concluded on your own that you didn't pass muster. (And from where did they get their standards?)

In 1991, the Dalai Lama was asked about self-worthiness by a western psychologist. Even though the Dalai Lama understands English very well, he had to ask several times for a translation. It seems that in Tibetan culture, the concept of self-unworthiness is unknown. It is a uniquely western affliction! We learn it!

So if you believe a thought that severely impairs how you approach life, and you don't even know if it is true, either you've never looked at it deeply, or you don't even know you are carrying the underlying belief. If you aren't sure whether something is true or not, stop and look at how believing such a thought affects how you live your life. Then you are free to decide if the show is worth the price of admission. If you continue to have the same unwanted experiences over and over again, it might be time to look at your deep-seated beliefs about the world and your place in it. (Perhaps consider that string of loser boyfriends.)

We can examine our beliefs one at a time. This is the lifelong learning program. Or we can just see through the whole game and notice that all thought that is not functional thought, objective self-inquiry, or creative thought is of no value in the awakening game and is simply not true in any ultimate sense.

"So how can I see through the whole of it at once?"

Excellent question!

Thoughts are strings of words in our minds. There was a time when we didn't know any words, and yet we were very much alive—just look into a newborn baby's eyes. As babies, we might have been unhappy to be experiencing a cold, wet diaper, but it didn't manifest in the mentation: "Where the hell is Mom? I'm freezing my buns off." Words to describe experiences were learned later.

Every word is a concept. The word "walk" isn't the same as putting one foot in front of another. The word "walk" conceptualizes the act of walking just like this sentence does. Therefore, no word can ever be the real thing. Reading the word "apple" is not the same as biting into a crisp, juicy, tangy fruit just picked from a tree on a cool, clear autumn morning. And the actual experience is infinitely more satisfying than the previous sentence could ever be.

And then we learn how to combine these (conceptual) words into sentences and combine sentences into complex beliefs and opinions, which we then somehow take to be real and true. God-like, we wave the magic wand of self-certainty over our thoughts and imbue them with reality! We transform these compounded word concepts—that can never be real—into statements that we believe contain ultimate truth. We are such accomplished magicians that we even fool ourselves!

So when we sit down and *try* to meditate (an oxymoron, by the way), we usually do one of two things: either we try really hard to stop thinking (at least about things that we don't want to think about), or we try to find that one true thought that will resolve everything—the proverbial needle in the hay bale. (No one makes haystacks anymore.)

"But if no thought is ultimately true, and if trying to stop thinking doesn't work, what can we poor seekers do?"

If you happen to be fortunate enough to get to this point of quandary where you (a) understand that thought happens beyond your control, and (b) realize that no thought is ultimately true, then you have reached the point where the following question can be meaningfully asked: "Does it really matter if my thought stream is present or not?" However, until you realize (a) and (b) are true in your own direct experience, you will remain condemned to the tyranny of thought and to the frustration of attempted meditation.

The thoughts I'm talking about here are the conditioned ones that have emotional baggage; that is, thought streams that we either love or hate. However, regardless of whether we are attracted or repelled, we are invested. These are the thoughts that hook us. The vast majority of people spend their lives in this stockade. You might call this variety of thoughts "thoughts with side effects." (Our minds should come with the kind of warnings you find in the fine print on pharmaceutical ads, like the ones for antidepressant remedies with suicidal thoughts as a side effect. Really?) Included in this type of thought pattern is any sentence that begins with judgmental phraseology such as: *he should, she should, they should, he shouldn't have, they shouldn't, I'm right, we're right, it's not right, they're wrong, if only, it's not fair, you make me, if it wasn't for, he deserves,* etc., etc., etc. These are all arguments with life: arguments with what has happened, arguments with what is happening, or arguments with what might happen in the non-existent future.

So, leaving aside functional thought, self-inquiry, and creative thought, why be bothered in the least by all your other thoughts? If none of them can ever be fundamentally true and if they pass through your mind of their own accord, is it necessary to spend hours, days, expensive weekend workshops, or lifetimes trying to get rid of them? No, thankfully, it's not.

An intelligent conclusion would be to see that these conditioned random thoughts are only automatic-pilot responses and of no inherent value. We can complain to our friends and acquaintances (and perhaps to strangers in the checkout line) about how messed up the world is, but we will never win the argument. God will not realize one day after hearing your complaints that She indeed made a terrible mistake and, in a flash, remake the world to conform to your view of how it should be. The world is how the world is. Only by accepting the actuality of what is happening do we have any chance of changing anything to any meaningful degree. By acknowledging how the world is, we become aligned with Reality. We are then freed from a disempowering argument with what is, and we can channel our energies into some real-life action, large or small, that we find ourselves compelled to do. Complaints are not helpful. They are not helpful to you and they are not helpful to anyone else. Complaints about the world won't resolve anything and actually *add* to the dysfunctionality of the world. *Do* something instead. Or, better yet, wake up and then choose to do something.

When we see, understand, and accept that thinking may be present or absent, but either way it is of little concern, then and only then will useless conditioned thought begin to subside. It may take some time, but what's the rush, if not just another thought? Only when you are no longer energizing nonfunctional thoughts with your attempts to hold onto the pleasant ones and reject the disturbing ones will the thinking mind begin to loosen its choke hold on your consciousness.

So, here's the stark truth: If you are waiting

for thinking to stop permanently and completely so that you can awaken, you are simply postponing your awakening by digging a moat in front of the gateless gate.

Why do we insist on believing that conceptual thought is a barrier to what is actually real and eternal and ever-present? Because we believe that some (maybe all!) of our beliefs are true. We doubt that we could survive without our beliefs. We are fascinated by our beliefs. We are attracted to and repelled by our beliefs. We enjoy them. We fear them. We give them power. We are like gods granting life to our favored beliefs. We wonder who we would be without our beliefs. We fear that the world is teetering on the brink and will fall apart completely if we were to relinquish our opinions about what is right and wrong with the world. We vainly believe that it is our fervently-held beliefs that are the collective linchpin holding life-as-we-know-it together.

I remember when I first entered Princeton, it seemed as if everyone except me had opinions about everything—sophisticated opinions; opinions they could defend; impregnable fortresses of beliefs. It all sounded so mature, so impressive. I felt like a naïve public school kid with no worldly smarts. I concluded, "I need to get me some of those opinions." I tried hard for many years to develop a set of beliefs that I could believe in—that I could trot out when the opportunity presented itself, but those opinions always seemed squishy—no solid footing anywhere. I envied certainty, but it proved elusive. I could not have imagined back then that the path would lead through total and complete uncertainty.

Nonfunctional thoughts, without one's energizing belief in them, fall of their own non-existent weight. Is it really a problem if they linger a while (or longer)? The Buddha taught, "The Dharma is beautiful in the beginning, beautiful in the middle, and beautiful in the end." Like making love. Relax. Let the river carry you to the sea. There is no need to try to swim faster than the river. Relax and enjoy the journey.

Find out what is conscious of those thoughts. Is that consciousness ever disturbed by a thought, or is disturbance only ever created by thoughts of what should, or shouldn't, be?

Even after awakening, thoughts will still come and go. It's not a problem unless we think it is. Sometimes a cloud drifts by and temporarily obscures the sun. When that happens, we don't doubt the existence of the sun. But if we become alarmed and believe the thought, "Oh, no, I've lost my awakeness because I am thinking again," we can again conjure up apparent unawakeness.

By insisting, "I must transcend all thought in order to awaken," we accomplish the impossible: we obscure the ever-present reality of our own True Nature.

Use your mind when you need it. It's useful. A hammer is useful. But just because you have a hammer and respect its usefulness, don't then believe that everything else must, therefore, be a nail. Use the right tool for the job at hand. When it's important to differentiate between things, the mind is great. However, if we're seeking Oneness, well then . . . a different approach is needed.

If we encounter an awesome sunset, it doesn't actually require us to comment, "What an awesome sunset." Better to allow ourselves to be awed speechless.

But, if our own mind or some other mind decides to comment on the sunset, no matter. Simply, recognize that the One Reality whose nature is consciousness is present whether or not thought is happening.

Thought can obscure the One Reality only if we let it.

But the One Reality is never absent.

And it can never be lost.

Because you are it.

# Myth #5
"I Have to Meditate—a Lot"

Stay with me on this one. I realize that this book is about misleading spiritual mythology, but let me clarify right away that meditation is a good thing. I wholeheartedly recommend it to anyone. It may not necessarily wake you up, but it will probably make you healthier, more balanced, more relaxed, and, in general, a nicer person to be around.

However, a meditation practice can go astray in three ways: (a) you can get overly focused on trying to perfect some technique, (b) you can believe that the goal of meditation is to visit elevated spiritual states, or (c) you can develop a spiritual identity as an accomplished meditator.

The first risk is to believe that you have to do something while you're meditating. You can't just sit there. As if we don't have enough to do already! The myth is that even while I am sitting alone in a quiet room with my eyes closed, I really should still be doing something—some goal-oriented enterprise. "Anything! Just tell me what to do. I'm willing to do anything at all as long as it's not nothing!"

And meditation is no small endeavor if you try to comply with all the advice you hear: Follow your breath. Count your breaths. Repeat a mantra all day, preferably a secret one. Light some incense. Don't fidget. Stop thinking. (Yeah, right.) Witness your thoughts. Love your thoughts. Look for the blue flame (or stare at a candle). Merge with the white light. Sit up straight in a hard-backed chair, or better yet, buy a zafu. Force your legs into a full Lotus. Hold your hands in the correct mudra. Wear the right clothing: organic, cotton, loose-fitting, of course. "Surely, it must be better to do something—anything—than to simply relax in a comfortable position in my easy chair!"

Countless ads have convinced us of "No pain, no gain." "You don't get something for nothing." "An idle mind is the devil's workshop." (I wonder what sinister mind came up with that little ditty!)

But if all that is happening for you is that you have gotten very good at practicing your chosen meditation technique, you might ask yourself, "Is this why I started to meditate —just to get good at sitting still and being able to count my breaths to one hundred?" If your goal is to become a world-class meditator, that's fine, but a more significant question might be: "Does my meditation method, or any meditation method, lead to sustained awakening?" By sustained awakening, I mean that there is abiding recognition that consciousness is fully present even when you are not sitting in meditation. If you've been meditating for many years and the answer to that question is still "No, not really" you might ask yourself if it seems reasonable that a technique that requires effort will result in something the Taoists have described as "the natural state." (It's not really a state—it's that within which all states come and go, and we all know, well most of us anyway, that the word "natural" has been totally corrupted by the processed-food industry and doesn't mean anything anymore, but you get the idea.)

If you've been practicing a meditation method for a long time, you might try—just as an experiment—sitting down in your favorite chair in any old comfortable position and simply noticing what is happening before you try to make anything happen. Ask yourself if consciousness is currently present. If it is not, stop reading and dial 911. However, if you are conscious, it is worth noting that consciousness is present *before* you started to try to meditate. From this simple recognition, make no attempt to control the mind or to direct its experience to reach any particular state. If the mind has been bottled up for a long time, when released it may get noisy when you first try this. Give it some time to settle. No rush. No goal. Be attentive, but not manipulative. You might discover that simple awareness is present before you go looking for it. No effort required. The goal is already accomplished. Why not give it a try? What do you have to lose—except perhaps a few decades of painful seeking?

The second way a meditation practice can go astray is if you believe that the goal of meditation is to experience altered states of consciousness, preferably ecstatic ones. Altered states, even elevated spiritual states, can only ever occur within consciousness—images projected onto the screen of consciousness. *You* are the screen, and experiences are the flickering of images projected onto that screen. Without consciousness, the movie doesn't exist. All experiences, all states, come and go, and none of these experiences is ultimately any more real than any other. Some might be more helpful, or more fun, or scarier, or more inspiring, but none have any more fundamental reality than any other. Even "spiritual" experiences are ultimately no more real than any other experience.

"Ordinary" consciousness within which everything is happening is the only true constant. Ordinary is extraordinary. Recognizing that as the truth of who *you* really are is the first glimpse of awakening. It is the doorway. It is not an altered state. It's not even a spiritual state! It is that within which all experiences or states occur. If you are using meditation to seek spiritual states, you may be successful in your search, but you may miss the significance of this (extra) ordinary, everyday awakeness. Which is to say that you've missed the entire point.

Plain, ordinary, everyday consciousness may not seem very exciting at first glance, but Truth doesn't have to prove its existence in a heavy-handed, in-your-face kind of way because, well, nothing else actually exists. If there are no competitors, the Infinite has no need to defend Itself. We, as humans, either realize the primacy of consciousness or not. Truth is willing to play along and let you think you are sitting in the driver's seat—imagining yourself as a separate entity living your own independent life in a great big (sometimes scary) world. But that is like those little plastic steering wheels they used to have on the passenger side of the car (before mandatory rear seat baby carriers) where young children could imagine they were driving the car.

If we believe that the goal of meditation is to reach elevated spiritual states consistently, or even at will, and we miss the ever-present immensity of consciousness, then we have allowed shiny trinkets to lure us off the path to awaken. Colored lights can hypnotize.

The third way that meditation may prove to be a diversion is to believe that you have to spend years and years on the cushion to realize its benefits. A consequence of this belief is that you think realization is closer at hand if you have spent decades meditating. Or conversely, you believe that you can't be anywhere near realization because you are a rookie meditator.

Either way, for the seasoned meditator or the newbie, this belief gets in the way. If you believe that you have to meditate a lot for many years in order to awaken, so shall it be. If you are a long-time meditator, you may get complacent about enlightenment: "This lifetime, next lifetime. What's the difference?" Or you might develop a well-polished, spiritual identity that you can roll out in public: "Yes, indeed I am an advanced spiritual person." Really? Regardless of how many hours you have spent meditating or how many visions you have enjoyed, if you believe that your spiritual practice has set you above and apart from others, you have not yet made it to first base.

On the other hand, if you have never meditated, you may believe that there is some hidden secret that's revealed only after long years of aching knees. And you miss the ever-present enlightenment that is just waiting patiently for you to notice her Grace in this moment.

If you believe that many years are necessary, then you logically believe that you are closer to awakening if you have twenty years of meditation under your belt than if you are just starting out. But what if that's not true? What if this meditate-to-awaken game doesn't work on the same principle as the old-fashioned, grade school punishment where you had to stay after school and write (longhand, mind you) one thousand times "I will not think bad thoughts" before you were allowed to go free?

When you do something for a long time, and especially when you get good at it, you can easily develop a sense of personal satisfaction in your accomplishment, maybe a little peer recognition, perhaps a little pride, and some self-identification can creep in: "Yes, it's true. I have become an accomplished spiritual meditator." You light incense when friends come over; you adopt a distant gaze; you speak and eat more slowly; you start wearing "Om" T-shirts or flimsy garments from your last trip to India. In your own mind, you begin to identify yourself as a spiritual and meditative person. Having a good, solid spiritual identity is as good as most identities and perhaps better than many, I suppose, except, of course, if the certainty of your righteousness increases your sense of separation from those heathen non-meditating, non-vegetarian, non-believers.

As a long-time meditator, you might ask yourself: "Am I free, or am I now a prisoner of my new identity?"

A caution here is that being a lifelong meditator is not a guarantee of anything. You may be no more enlightenment-prone than an innocent, openhearted first-timer who inquires deeply without preconceptions and with utter sincerity.

At any moment, you are either awake, or you are functioning from your conditioning. Do not presume that the number of years of meditation practice counts.

So, of all the millions of life-long meditators in the last few thousand years, how many woke up? I have no idea, but if I had to guess I would say a lot more than we know about and a lot less than anyone would call favorable odds. So how do those odds compare to waking up out of dead-end drunkenness, or out of abject suffering, or waking up while walking across the parking lot and noticing a cloud? Or waking up while driving through a town called Boring, Oregon (no kidding, there is such a town) coming home from work late at night sipping Port straight out of the bottle? Do you know? I don't either.

My point is not to recommend alcoholism as a path to awakening (unless, of course, you have already committed yourself to that particular path). I am also certainly not suggesting voluntarily practicing depression or drinking while driving. I am suggesting that we don't have a clue what will wake us up, so it is essential to remain alert and engaged, whether meditating or not. Awakening will come in whatever package is necessary to penetrate our thoroughly conditioned minds. If meditation relieves you of some of your conditioning, then great! However, if meditation is only creating a pretty new identity and adding to your armor, well then ... stop doing that!

Now, before going any further, it seems only fair to point out that meditation is a good way to relax, especially if you aren't busy trying to achieve something like, oh . . . I don't know, let's just say enlightenment. And meditation is an excellent way, if you're paying attention, to notice the machinations of your mind. When meditating, you may notice that your mind has a mind of its own. You may notice that it is one big run-on sentence that you can't turn on and off and that goes off in directions you'd rather not go and sometimes gets lost in a daydream about the silliest of things and then you suddenly remember what your best friend said about you the other day that was totally unprovoked and not really true at all, and she's not all that perfect either—oh, wait a minute, speaking of perfection, I'm supposed to be meditating and not having all of these thoughts, in fact, I was planning on meditating earlier this morning but decided to sleep in instead and had the most wonderful dream about . . . . If you've ever meditated, you know that the previous sentence is an exaggeration only in its brevity. "When is that bell going to ring anyway? What do you mean we've only been meditating for five minutes?"

Perhaps the most instructive thing about meditation is that you get to notice "up close and personal" that you have no control over your thoughts. However, if you are paying attention, you notice that each thought enters consciousness and then, at some point, leaves consciousness. And, occasionally, if you are really paying attention, you may notice a very brief gap before another thought begins. In this small gap, thought is absent. Yet *you* still exist. I repeat: thought is absent but you are not. Contemplate the significance of this gap. In this gap, you have no history, no age, no profession, no particular gender, no grievances, no parents, no problems, nothing. Yet you exist! This is big, folks.

Decartes wrote the famous phrase, "I think therefore I am." Notice, however, that you don't vaporize in a puff when your thinking pauses for a moment. You may also notice that babies are perfectly alive even though words are not yet flowing through their heads. In fact, some of the times when we feel most alive is when there is no thought stream happening, like when we are surprised by the punchline of a good joke, or at the moment of sexual orgasm, or when we are stunned into awe by a humpback whale unexpectantly breaching nearby. So an alternative explanation of our fundamental nature is needed. I suggest: "consciousness exists therefore I am." Without consciousness, there is no thought, no you, and no world, which makes consciousness sound pretty fundamental to me. It's not an absolutely true statement (no statement is), but perhaps it's an improvement on Decartes.

However, before we jump to conceptual conclusions about the primacy of consciousness, what we can say with certainty is that *whatever it is that you are* continues to exist in the absence of thought. Hmm . . . . Now that is a giant clue right there!

If whatever it is *you* are remains when thought

is absent, then:

*You* cannot be a thought.

Any thought!

Any concept! (because any concept is just a grouping of related thoughts)

Any belief! (because all beliefs are simply concepts imbued with certainty)

Any dogma! (because dogma is an adopted set of beliefs)

Any religion! (because religions, by definition, are a set of beliefs and dogmas)

This is an extraordinarily valuable insight if you are looking to find out who you are. You don't have to spend years sorting through all possible concepts to find the one true concept that defines who or what you are. If the answer doesn't exist in thought, you can avoid the daunting prospect of spending a thousand lifetimes sifting through an infinite number of thoughts and concepts in hopes of finding the one true thought/belief/concept/opinion/dogma/religion that will finally make sense of everything.

Thoughts are concepts. *You* are not a concept. *You* cannot be a concept since a concept is nothing more than a man-made fabrication. And you are more than that. Infinitely more.

As long as you're meditating anyway and have plenty of time on your hands, a useful question to ask is, "Who/what is the one who is meditating?" It may become obvious that the answer to that question cannot be a thought or a concept. Who *you* are cannot be condensed into a thought. Who/what *you* really are is beyond all thought, so it's a complete waste of time to try to define yourself conceptually or historically or hypothetically or speculatively. (By the way, just so you have an idea of where the whole thing is headed, who *you* really are is also not limited by your body, your emotions, time, space, the duality of good and bad, or the Universe as we commonly know it.)

When the *non-conceptual* answer to the question "Who is it that's trying to meditate?" dawns, it's game over. Life will never look quite the same again.

That doesn't mean that you have to stop

thinking in order to be who *you* really are. And you don't have to become something that you are not already. You just have to notice what you *already* are. Who *you* are is not limited by thought. Who *you* are is who *you* are regardless of the thoughts passing through your mind.

If you are honest with yourself, you cannot control your thoughts anyway, so why bother to identify yourself with any thought—good or bad? Let thoughts come and go. Why take credit for the "good" ones and burden yourself with blame for the "bad" ones?

No thought, sentence, book, treatise, catchy phrase, or concept is absolutely true. The vibrant reality of Life cannot be contained within finite little boxes called words.

Don't take my word for it. Find out for yourself. It may sound like relinquishing conceptual thought is giving away something of great value. It is not. Have your beliefs to date proved liberating or imprisoning? Not having to determine your relationship to the latest news event, or your judgment of your neighbor, or what so-and-so should be doing or not doing is incredibly liberating of one's energy. I don't mean liberating in the sense that it is OK to go out and do stupid things; you just cease being imprisoned by self-limiting beliefs. Then each moment is fresh and unique and joyful—regardless of what is happening.

Ask yourself, "Is this belief true? Who would I be without this belief? How would my life change if I didn't have this belief? And, do I really want to continue to pay the price that I am paying to hold on to this belief?" (Byron Katie is a wonderful resource when you're in the mood for demolishing beliefs.)

When you first meditate, you may notice only an occasional and very brief gap of stillness between the run-on sentences of the mind. No matter. Go with what you have been given. Be grateful for the small gaps. But avoid the temptation to conclude that gaps are good and thoughts are bad. Eventually, if you are really, really paying attention, you may notice that the stillness that is *you* is present whether or not thoughts are happening. Again, you can't *make* this happen because it is *already* happening. This is not an attainment; it is just noticing the truth of what is always effortlessly occurring.

This noticing-what-is-already-happening-without-trying-to-make-something-different-happen is a supremely worthwhile practice that has no goal and requires no effort other than simply observing what is already happening in your own direct, firsthand experience. I know this instruction does not sound difficult enough to be the entrance point to liberation, but who said that this awakening thing has to be hard? (OK. Some people say that. But do they know what they are talking about? Or is their agenda served by making it sound difficult? Perhaps they have a multilevel program with escalating tuition fees as you progress to ever more secret levels?)

Even if you choose meditation as a path, keep your eyes open (figuratively) and be willing to ask yourself from time to time, "Is this working?" The journey to awaken is not about becoming more peaceful and happier although that may happen and, ultimately, it is not even personal to you; it is fundamentally a path of undoing what you think you are and what you think you know in order to be empty enough for Life to flow through you with minimal impedance.

Adyashanti summarizes the journey as follows: "The spiritual task we are given is a simple one: to attend to that inner spark of radiance, to hold vigil over it until we realize it to be ourself, and to dig up and cast off any argument we have with its love."

Undoing untruth can be liberating, but it can also be painful. It doesn't have to be painful—it more or less depends on how tightly you are holding on to your story.

Your best bet is to let go and enjoy the ride. Let go entirely, and the ride home is over.

Awakening only requires an instant of letting your guard down. If it takes thirty years of meditation to get to that point, then great—it was thirty years well spent. If it happens while reading this sentence, even better! And I guarantee that the next thirty years will be a lot more enjoyable.

Formal meditation is fine, but don't let it lull you into another dream. It is a tool. Use it. When the project is finished, you can let it go. You might still meditate for the simple joy of it, but then the whole of Life will be like effortless meditation—the dreamer and the dream dancing together and laughing.

And all is well.

# Myth #4
"I Need to Get Rid of My Ego"

To examine this myth, a useful question to ask right from the get-go is, "What is it in myself that wants to get rid of my ego?" If you are being honest with yourself, you can see that there is an agenda at play here. You want to make a trade: ego for enlightenment. You wouldn't give up your ego otherwise, would you? Not really. If truth be known, we sort of like our egos. They can give us a great deal of pleasure sometimes, like when the Universe cooperates and we get what we want. And after all, for better or for worse, we've spent our whole lives nurturing our ego, fretting over it, consoling it, and trying to improve it. If we're going to trade it in, we certainly don't want to just give it away, do we? We want to get something of equal or greater value in return! We imagine that we're willing to make a trade, but only if we can trade up. And we convince ourselves that we're on such a noble journey to enlightenment!

So, who is it that wants to get rid of ego? Who is this "who" that wants to gain something in the trade (enlightenment, or spiritual powers, or even just plain old peace of mind)? Let's see ... a "who" that is scheming to gain something for itself. What could that be ... hmm? Let's see, maybe ... ego? This is ego imagining it can be a new and improved ego if it can only just transcend ego. How clever! Ego may not be real, but that's not to say that it isn't just about the cleverest thing around.

So what exactly is ego? I'm sure there are much more sophisticated clinical definitions out there, but to me (irony intended), it's just that vague sense of me-ness. That muddled mass of thoughts and beliefs and memories and storylines and sensations and emotions and hopes and fears and dreams. The conglomerate I've come to think of as "me." Of course, I might think highly of myself one minute and then despair over my unworthiness the next. My ego is nothing if not creative, but nevertheless, I somehow work this inconsistency into the concretized idea of the triumvirate that's at the center of the known Universe: me, myself, and I. The Trinity of my realm!

Let's start with what we know. There is this bodymind that I wake up "in" (apparently) every morning. It's true that this body is where I seem to be observing from. But wouldn't I need a body with eyes and ears and maybe a few other senses in order to observe anything?

We don't need to own a car to drive one. We can lease one, rent one, borrow one, or steal one. In any event, to assume that we *are* the vehicle just because we're driving it is no more than a flimsy assumption. Just because nearly everyone believes something doesn't mean that it's true. At one time, everyone believed that the Earth was the center of the Universe around which the Heavens circled. You could get yourself imprisoned, or worse, if you even questioned that assumption. Today, you people might think you are a nincompoop (I'm not sure exactly that means but I like the sound of the word) if you doubt the reality of your separate self, but at least they won't burn you at the stake. Lucky us!

So the fact that this sensing organism (our MBU) exists doesn't necessarily prove that we inhabit that MBU as a separate self. I admit that is what we all assume is true. But do you *know* that it's true? Remember: belief is not your friend in the awakening game.

So, isn't the belief that I must get rid of ego before I can awaken just another competing thought within the noisy arena of my head? Of course, there are other countering thoughts, such as "Who would I be without my ego?" (This is an excellent question, by the way.) Or, "How do I know everything will be OK if my ego drops off the edge of the planet into nothingness?" (You don't. This is where faith comes in; not faith-in-something, just objectless faith, or faith in Life as a whole.) Or, "Although it can be a pain in the ass sometimes, I have gotten comfortable with how well I've polished my ego over the years, and come to think of it, I'm not so sure I want to give it up." (Ah... now, we're telling the truth!)

The only thing that wants to get rid of ego is ego—one thought -competing with another. And, thus, if we try to get rid of it, a lifetime of inner conflict and mental maneuvering (and expensive workshops) ensues. All it takes is one simple belief to obscure the ever-present Infinite and the belief that we need to get rid of ego will certainly suffice.

Meanwhile, consciousness is sitting back in the bleachers watching the whole game, attentive, amused and curious, but undisturbed by the whole drama.

The reason that ego feels sticky enough to cause us to contemplate a project to rid ourselves of it is that we've been taught, and now believe, that our ego, our "me," is real. That, my friends, is the mother of all beliefs, the whopper of a tale we tell ourselves (and, in all innocence, convey our children and they to their children—not in so many words, but in our whole-hearted participation in the almost universally accepted illusion). We're whistling in the dark trying desperately to keep the truth of ourselves at bay, and we don't even know that we're doing it.

Consciousness has been fused together with this idea of a "me." It happened at a very young age. And we have not questioned it since. We believe that we're limited to the sum of our thoughts, emotions, history, hopes, and fears packaged in our skin-encased Mind Body Units. And then we conclude that this fragile little MBU *is* what's conscious. But do we *know* that, or are we just making that assumption because that's what everyone else believes? Could it be that we are suffering from a simple, innocent case of mistaken identity?

You may say, "But this "me" feels so solid,

so individual, and so personal. I even have this unique body that 'I' wake up 'in' every morning." I grant you that it certainly feels like that, but it feels like that because we were taught that's how it is. But there is something odd. Even the language is a little odd when you consider it closely. We refer to *my* body, *my* personality, *my* emotions, *my* thoughts. But where exactly is the "me" in all of those "mys"? Can you find it?

We can get all Freudian and refer to it as my ego, but that's just giving a name to a concept. It's like scientists giving the name "gravity" to the phenomena of our feet being pulled towards the ground. Scientists can't say what gravity actually is, mind you; they can only measure its effects on things. Ego is similar. Psychologists create a term like "ego" to make it sound all scientific-y. We assume that they must know what they're talking about—they're scientists after all. So we take possession of the concept, imagine that we're on a deep inner journey, and create intimacy at the same time by working on "my ego." Now we have a conceptual entity ("me") possessing another conceptual entity ("ego")—a "me" pondering my sense of me-ness. A hierarchy of conceptual entities! A Ponzi scheme empowered only by our belief in it. Let's avoid this tiresome regression-of-identities game. Let's just define ego as that vague sense of me-ness and move on.

So again, the question: Where does this me-ness/ego reside? Have you ever found it? Is there some finite entity inside there somewhere—anywhere? A mini-me perhaps? Some Oz pulling the levers of your life? Have you ever looked behind the curtain? If you have, did you ever find anything that wasn't just another concept, memory, thought, emotion, or experience?

It seems like a solid "I" should be in there somewhere. "Certainly, the leading actor in my life ("me") must exist—somewhere, anywhere!" It seems utterly ridiculous even to question that seemingly obvious fact. "They might lock me up if I let on that *I* am on a journey looking for *me*." "Why even bother to look when there are so many more interesting things to do?" "After all, isn't deciding what opinion I should have with regard to the evening news-de-jour far more significant than trying to find out what this "I" thing is that we refer to a thousand times every day? "Maybe one day I'll look under the hood—when I have more time, when I'm not so busy." Or maybe, we don't really want to know. After all, who knows what boogeymen might be lurking there in those shadows?

But the odd thing is, when we finally get up the gumption (one of my grandmother's favorite words) to go looking for that little me/ego fellow inside, he/she/it turns out to be surprisingly elusive. We can look for a very long time and not find it. We can find all kinds of debris it leaves behind: all the difficult memories; all the grudges; all the hopes, fears, old un-met dreams, new dreams, fantasies, blames, shames, guilts, hatreds, resentments, a tattered flag of pride here and there, fortresses of arrogance, etc., etc., etc. But where is this me-ness/ego itself? Surely, it's in there somewhere.

Take your time with this paragraph. It will probably seem silly and repetitive, but humor me if you would. Go slowly, step by step, and feel your own sense of it at each step. I suggest that you sense into these questions with your body, not with your thinking apparatus. OK, here goes (with a nod to Fred Davis): Does this "me-ness" reside in your legs? (I know you can see where this is going, but stay with me.) How about your lower torso? Does your me-ness reside exclusively there? I know a lot of people like to *function* from that region, but that's not what I'm asking. This isn't a biology quiz. Again, it's just your own felt sense of where that "me" entity resides. How about your upper torso? I know your heart is there and a few chakras and the seat of emotions and all that. For a moment, please forget what you think you know and just go with your actual internal experience at this moment. OK, that leaves just the head, which is where, initially, you probably guessed home base would be. We've been taught that thoughts occur there—command central as it were. Right now, it doesn't matter what we were taught; all that counts is our actual firsthand experience. So is your sense of "I" confined to the brain, or is it not quite that specific? Is it delineated by your scalp, or is it more vaguely in the vicinity of your head? Remember, I'm not talking biology here. Your own experience is the only thing that counts. Sense into it. You are your own expert here. So:

In that sense of "I," can you find any actual little entity in there, or does it feel more like a field of awareness?

Is there any "thingness" to it, or is it difficult to assign any attributes to it?

Does it have a sharp edge—a limit beyond which it doesn't exist, or when you gaze out into the room, does that field of awareness seem to encompass the whole room?

In your lifetime, has this sense of spaciousness aged? (I understand that the *content* has changed, but here I am talking about just the "I" sense of this spaciousness itself.)

OK, here's a tough one: Does that field of

awareness itself have a history, a story?

Has that spaciousness always been there? Can you remember a time when it wasn't?

Has that spaciousness changed over time? Or has it always been conscious of whatever was happening at every moment—conscious of our daydreams, or thoughts, our experiences, our dreams at night, and everything else.

OK, if you played along and really allowed yourself to feel into these questions in your own direct experience, you just transcended ego and discovered (or re-discovered) the limitless consciousness that is beyond time and space. Nice going! No heavy lifting required.

If you played within the parameters, I would wager confidently that you didn't find a non-conceptual "me" entity, but perhaps you did encounter an awareness that is not confined to the body, that is spacious, and that is unaffected by the passage of time. Hmm . . . limitless, formless, eternal. Could this field of consciousness be what *you are?* Does it have a sense of *I-Amness* to it?

Not I am this or I am that—just a sense of I am. It's your experience; you tell me.

The Zen folks call it no-thing-ness (also spelled "nothingness") because it is not a thing. We can't stand back from it and look at it because it's what's doing the looking. If you like English grammar, you could say that it is the ultimate subject. Or you could say that it is like the eye which can see things but cannot see itself. Sometimes it is called emptiness because it is empty of attributes and empty of all that "me" content. It's what's aware of the "me" content.

Christians might call it the Fullness of Being because it is not exactly empty at all—it is indeed aliveness itself.

Via Negativa. Via Positiva. Two paths, same ultimate understanding.

The me-ness/ego is just a bundle of thoughts, each of which comes and goes. But when we keep thoughts and experiences continuously in play by rapid mental juggling, there is apparent continuity. I know I'm dating myself to the predigital age here, but bubble gum used to come with little paper booklets that had static pictures on each page, but when you flipped through the pages quickly, the figures appeared to move. The moving image was imaginary (as it is in movies). When we look back on our past, we remarkably retain a belief that we can remember our lives in a smooth continuum from a young age to the present moment. But if we look closely, we can remember only occasional, brief video clips and have forgotten everything else. (If you doubt this, try to remember what happened to you while you were in seventh grade. I don't mean general statements like "my best friend was named Bill" or "I went to Muddling Middle School." I mean actual specific events that you can replay like a video clip in your mind. Can you get to ten for the whole year? How about five? I suppose your answer might depend on your current age, but perhaps you understand my point, or you will soon enough.

Experiences are short-lived, memories fade,

and the body eventually (or sooner) declines. Consciousness is the one "thing" (actually a no-thing), the sole constant, that has witnessed everything that's ever happened to you throughout your entire life. Everything else has changed: your body has aged, your opinions have changed many times, your relationships have perhaps come and gone, your responsibilities have ebbed and flowed, your hairdo has gone through many improvements, you were a child and now you may have children, etc., etc.

But consciousness has been there as the star witness the whole time. So, let's ask it a few questions:

Has that spacious field of awareness ever been hurt? Or has it only witnessed painful events happening?

Has it been tarnished by anything you ever did, or thought, or by anything that has ever happened to you? (I'm not saying that bad things have not happened to you; I'm asking whether that spacious awareness itself was diminished.)

Has it ever been ill? Is it now ill?

Is it not as pristine as the day you were born?

These questions are not meant to distance or to disassociate yourself from reality; they are meant to induce a realization that who we are fundamentally is not limited to what we've always thought we were.

If you spent some time with the above questions, you can understand why it's sometimes referred to as "Pure Consciousness." The term "Pure" does not mean that you have to live a flawless life to experience it, and it does not refer to some spiritually elevated form of consciousness. The term refers to that field of consciousness itself and not to the content of that field. It is called "pure" because it cannot be harmed or hurt or tainted in any way and never has been. It is the context itself. *The context contains the content.*

You could also call it awareness—not awareness of something, just awareness—without an object of awareness and without a subject/object relationship with life. Loch Kelly calls it "awake awareness," which calls attention to its aliveness. It is not removed from Life; it is the very essence of Life.

Everything that happens and everything that we think and feel appears on this screen of awareness/consciousness. Even thoughts and concepts about who we think we are consist of nothing more than images projected onto this screen of consciousness.

Ego is not a problem because it's not actually real. It's only our belief in it that makes it seem real. Another way to say the same thing is that the you that you think you are is not real; the you that you think you are does not actually exist.

OK, there, I've said it—the deep, dark secret of true spirituality.

If you conclude that I must be writing this chapter from the funny pharm, I understand. But I'm not asking you to believe what I am saying. I'm only suggesting that you look for yourself. Here's a (deceptively) easy three-step program to do just that:

Step One: Allow yourself to let go of your certainty about who or what you imagine yourself to be. Simply hold it as an open question. Or admit: "Since I've never actually looked, I don't actually know if there is a finite 'me' inside there somewhere or not." This is called being honest with oneself.

Step Two: Drop into that felt sense of where your being-ness seems to reside like you did in the thought exercise above. Don't try to understand what it means. Don't look for a big spiritual experience. Don't indulge in conceptualizing about it. For a while, it's probably best not to try to explain it to your friends or even your lover (and especially not your boss.) Let it mature. It may start out to be a seemingly minor realization, but don't let first appearances fool you. It is the doorway home. God is not "out there." There is no "out there" out there.

Step Three: Repeat Step Two. I'm not joking. Everyone misses the doorway because they are in a rush to get on to something more fascinating, because they are looking for the sparkly enticements of the spiritual realm. If you look where awakening is not, you will look forever. Stay with Step Two until that sense of being-ness is there no matter what else is happening. Sometimes it may be in the foreground; sometimes it can be in the background. But notice that it is never absent.

Could this plain, ordinary, everyday consciousness be what you are? Could it really be that simple? Could it be a done-deal already?

This is why seeking always leads us astray. Seeking is always looking outside of our true self. Even thoughts and feelings are external to our true self. Because it is consciousness doing the looking, no matter which way we look, we never find enlightenment.

At first, you may only get a glimpse or you may only get it conceptually. That's OK. It's a beginning—a crack in your armor. Allow the sense of it to deepen. Be willing to feel into the truth of it. Be courageous enough to look with sincerity into your own direct experience without the crutches of theory, beliefs, and concepts.

It may take a while—maybe even several years—for identity to shift irreversibly from thinking of itself as a "me" to actually living from consciousness—even after the fact of our own True Nature is realized. But what's a couple years when that which is eternal has already been revealed?

It's actually the simplicity of it all that causes most people to overlook it. Many encounter it, immediately dismiss it, and continue searching. "It couldn't be that easy, could it?" Yes, it could be, and it is.

The mind loves complexity. Don't grant your mind sovereign reign in the journey of awakening. The mind will always have more questions. The mind will never be convinced. The mind will never understand to its full satisfaction. As long you grant your mind the role of ultimate judge of what is true, you will remain condemned to wandering aimlessly in the desert of thought.

Trust your instincts more.

Look within for the nonconceptual reality and trust what you find.

Trust Life.

Go all in.

You have nothing to lose but your false self.

# Myth #3

"Cool Spiritual Experiences Are Evidence of My Progress"

All experiences come and go. Each experience has a life span. When the experience is over, you are left with a memory. Ramana Maharshi told us: "Let come what comes, and let go what goes. Find out what remains." He knew that all experiences are impermanent, and he was pointing beyond to that which is not subject to experiential comings and goings. Examples of transient experiences can be as simple as your next thought, as profound as your birth and death, or as ecstatic as your next spiritual experience.

Spiritual experiences can be transformative, blissful, otherworldly, out-of-body, challenging, incapacitating, energetic, timeless, insightful, fulfilling, or countless other flavors. They may change how you view yourself and how you see the world. They may make you a nicer person to be around—even for yourself—and they may deepen your understanding of the way life works.

But the one thing that all experiences have in common, even spiritual experiences, is that they come, and then they go. After they pass, you may have a wonderful story to tell your friends, and you may bask in the wonder of the remembered experience. But in its retelling or remembering, it never has quite the same power or the same feeling of truth as it did when it was happening.

I once had a revelatory experience that was triggered by an old-timey country-and-western song I was listening to while driving to work. I still like the song, and I can still describe the experience (and will if anyone cares to listen). But it no longer conjures up the all-encompassing bliss (and roaring belly laughter) I experienced that day in 2005 when I realized that what *I am* is not separate from the cloud in the sky, the metal fence post by the side of the road, or anything else.

But the spiritual seeker thinks, "OK, that last spiritual experience was amazing, but here I am again, back here in my same old skin with my same old problems. As great as I thought that last spiritual experience was at the time, it apparently was not THE EXPERIENCE that will catapult me into a state of permanent bliss. But I'm hoping that maybe the next one will be." And, alas, the seeker is alive and well and off on another expectant journey.

Why do we believe that some experience (in the future, of course) will result in a permanent state of awakeness? Because we have assumed (or have been taught) that enlightenment is the result of having the *right* experience or, even worse, that enlightenment is one long (presumably forever), blissful, ecstatic, high, otherworldly, powerful experience from which we never come down.

Doesn't that sound like every druggie's dream?

Since we tend to judge our own happiness by the quality of the experiences we are having, we assume that enlightenment must be like when we feel good—only infinitely better. That sounds logical, but awakening doesn't cater to human logic—thankfully!

Awakening is about liberation from the incessant pull/push of desire and aversion. Awakeness is the ongoing realization that *you* (as *you* really are) are the consciousness that is conscious of the experience, regardless of whether that experience is mundane or spiritual, boring or ecstatic. And I'm not talking about some imaginary witness figure that we conjure up in our minds in order to stay detached from the world, hold our problems at a distance, and yet somehow remain in control. Consciousness is not a better version of "me," a lofty mental position, or a philosophical concept. It is that without which the world does not exist.

The algebraic equation is simple: If no consciousness, then no you and no world. Consciousness is primary.

Consciousness is not, therefore, a small thing. Actually, it is not a thing at all. Nor is it a state of mind. It has no shape, content, size, age, gender, or center, and yet it is never absent. That sounds like a riddle. Actually, many sly teachers have pointed to it in the form of a riddle: "Who are you?" At first encounter, that directive sounds easy enough. After all, seemingly, we have been who we assume we are for as long as we can remember. The difficulty arises when you actually take the bait and, for once, go looking for *you*. Surprisingly, *you* are nowhere to be found. How odd! So you look deeper. And deeper. Still no *you*. "But my teacher told me to find the real me, so it must be in there somewhere!" You get frustrated. You think you've failed. Maybe you try harder. Maybe you give up. But then sooner or later you go and buy some inexpensive book about spiritual awakening that you think might do the trick only to find out the author is telling you that you don't actually exist as a separate person. "That can't be right. I'll go buy another book."

Although consciousness is no small thing, it is so commonplace that we continuously, and unconsciously, dismiss its significance. We ignore this eternal, ever-present, inherently contented consciousness, and we go off seeking the next (hopefully more powerful!) spiritual experience. That path looks more glitzy. We are like the aboriginal jungle dweller when first encountering Western civilization; we are entranced by sparkly, mysterious objects.

Why do we believe the myth that spiritual experiences are indicative of pending enlightenment? Because it seems reasonable and because we like to think we are making progress toward our goal. Plus it feels good. We imagine we know what enlightenment will look like, and we assume that the journey toward it will happen in a logical, linear way like other goals that we've attained in our life. We expect to see progress toward some distant finish line—and feel better and better as we go. It makes sense, right? A string of increasingly powerful spiritual experiences sounds a heck of a lot more enjoyable than the neti, neti (not this, not that) path to awakening, or inquiring our way through countless false images of ourselves. We like fun and easy; it's the American way!

So we conclude that, "Yes, the last spiritual experience seemed powerful at the time, but I am certain that the next one will be better." We think that the third time will be the charm, or maybe more accurately, the 333rd time. How often does Lucy have to snatch the football away before Charley Brown catches on? Awakening is not an experience! It's not even a spiritual experience. It's what notices the spiritual experience and what notices the mundane experience that inevitably follows.

I once knew someone who had undeniable spiritual powers and who once told me, "I may have some faults in this world, but in the Other

World, I am Royalty." And my unspoken response was, "What notices that you have faults in this world and are treated like Royalty in the Other World? And is it not the same awareness operating in both worlds? Do not experiences in the Other World come and go just like they do in this world? So, then, which is more primary: the experiences or the consciousness within which those experiences occur?"

If we believe that spiritual experiences are indicative of our spiritual progress, we will devote our attention to finding just the right experience or ever more powerful experiences. We may have lots of spiritual experiences, and yet we may totally miss the ever-present reality of our True Nature.

The best way to miss finding something is to seek it where it is not. There's a wonderful story about Mullah Nasruddin, an ancient Persian sage/fool, who once lost his keys at night and was down on his hands and knees looking for them under a street lamp. A stranger came by and, after hearing of Nasruddin's predicament, also got down on his knees and started looking. After twenty minutes, the stranger asked Nasruddin where Nasruddin last saw his keys. Nasruddin said, "Well, I dropped them over there in the alley, but there's much better light to look for them here under this street lamp."

Someone may have a long resume of spiritual powers and incredible tales of travels in strange lands. Someone else may be a spiritual rookie. Neither is at any advantage or disadvantage when it comes to awakening. For long-time mystically inclined seekers, that may not be good news. However, the initial awakening needs only a split second for us to let our guard down and drop our insistence that we are separate from the rest of Existence. And that opportunity is always present. Your True Nature is alive and well and just waiting for you to notice.

If spiritual experiences happen, enjoy them, learn from them, allow yourself to be transformed by them, see how they impact your life, and let 'em go. As Adyashanti advised me, "Be grateful, and move on." The journey, if we can use that term, is ever onward. If your journey takes you to far-off lands, enjoy the scenery, but remember where your true home is, and the trip will be infinitely more enjoyable.

Even after your awakening matures, trees still look like trees, and you can still find the vegetable aisle in the local grocery store. But your perspective will be altered forever. You will no longer live in an "us-and-them" kind of world. Loving your neighbor as yourself will not require effort because you realize that your neighbor actually cannot be other than who *you* are. You will finally be able to be in a deep, intimate, and fearless relationship with a loved one because you will have discovered that there is nothing inside you that requires protection. Drama bores you, so you don't seek it out. In short, you no longer tend to squander your resources, and your life energy is freed to do the important stuff. Notice that I intentionally left this vague because I have no idea what "important stuff" you, specifically, are here in this life to do after you wake up. I do know that no one else is as uniquely qualified as you to be you and to do whatever it is that you are here to do, to see, and to learn.

Upon true awakening, seeking ends, but another journey begins. Experiences will still come and go. Enjoy them. They are called Life. Allow them to come when they come and let them go when they go.

Reside in what remains.

You will be home at last.

# Myth #2

"Awakening Is an Achievement"

Before awakening, it's common to believe that it will be a grand achievement when we reach the Promised Land—a (big) feather in our spiritual cap.

Of course, we don't usually say this out loud, but secretly, this is what we believe. It is a common, but dangerous belief—dangerous in the sense that it can confuse and mislead us at a critical moment in the journey.

Through effort, we have probably achieved many other things in life. Maybe we courted and won the mate of our dreams, or became successful in the workplace, or played sports well, or saved our pennies and bought the house we always wanted, or learned how to play the piano, or learned how to grow orchids that actually yield flowers. Or maybe our efforts were in a different direction. Maybe we started out as a novice drinker, and after putting in the long hours and suffering the innumerable hangovers that this path demands, we progressed to become much admired by our fellow bar mates as a seasoned drinker with a raspy voice and a varicosed nose. In either case, we are familiar with the linearity of striving for and finally attaining something.

If we choose positive goals, it is normal to visualize what it will be like when we reach our goal. It helps to motivate us on a long, arduous journey. We imagine how our life will be enhanced when we finally win the big one. We project the reward of happiness, respect, fame, glory, whatever.

Note that the reward is not so much the goal in itself. Rather, it's how we imagine we'll *feel* (happy, safe, respected, etc.) when we achieve the goal. This is a significant distinction and worthy of pondering. For example, what if you realized that it's not necessary to make a million dollars in order to "achieve" happiness, or to feel safe? What if you discovered that what you truly are is already completely content and beyond harm? Would you keep on working quite so hard? Hospice workers report that no one on their death bed ever says, "I wish I had worked longer hours."

We logically project that the journey to awaken will work in a similar progressive fashion as these other endeavors in our life. In our striving to awaken, we expect that we will pass goal posts along the way that will confirm our progress. We expect that we'll begin to ease into a state of ever-greater peace and increasing clarity and happiness. We expect our problems will gradually diminish. We expect people will understand what we are doing and why we are doing it.

And it may work like that for a while. (Well, probably not the last one about other people understanding what we are doing, particularly if those other people are family members or long-time friends or anyone who knew you when you wore nappies.) But, in the end at the key moment, when the whole game is on the line, it may feel like nothing is working anymore, like your life has not improved, like you are getting nowhere, and you may be tempted to conclude that the whole spiritual journey has been for naught. Spiritual techniques, like centering or even meditating to quiet the mind that may have often worked in the past, may not help anymore. At this point, you can be tempted to throw in the towel, head for the showers, and give up the whole search in frustration. (Note that, in such a case, you won't actually give up seeking; you will just look somewhere else for what will make you happy. Hmm... perhaps a quart of double chocolate fudge ice cream to start with.)

However, it is exactly at this point where the myth that awakening is some kind of grand achievement gets in the way—big time. If we conceptualize awakening as an achievement, and if the pursuit of it begins to lapse into apparent failure, then we can easily conclude "Well, I guess that enlightenment thing wasn't real after all," or "I gave it a good shot," or "I've got better things to do with my time," or "Maybe I'm just not the spiritual type," or perhaps even "I always knew I was unworthy." But it's often exactly at this point when the veil is thinnest, and you are closest to seeing through it.

At this point, if you are lucky, you will no longer be able to convince yourself that any other pursuit has the potential to transport you into a state of perpetual happiness or make sense out of life or be completely satisfying. You will have exhausted the alternatives. You will have no options left. There is nowhere to turn. Your defenses are down. You've run out of hope (a four-letter word, by the way).

It is at exactly this point that the sappy "darkest before dawn" metaphor may be appropriate.

This myth that awakening is an achievement is not just a harmless little plaything; it can derail the whole process of awakening if you believe it and are subject to its implications. You can be sorely tempted to give up at exactly the moment when it is essential to "keep going."

The idea of pushing further at this point goes against every survival instinct you have. It makes no sense. You can't conjure up any rational reason to go further. You can no longer inspire yourself with yet another carrot. You are played out.

However, I'm making the assumption that, if you're still reading this book, you are already committed to a journey from which you—as you have known yourself—will not return. There's a wonderful Buddhist expression: "being caught in the tiger's mouth." At first glance, this expression can sound alarming. However, it's actually a good thing. The wisdom of no escape is your friend. When everything in you may want to run away, realizing that escaping is no longer an option can yield a certain level of peace. The simplicity of having no choice is actually of enormous benefit because it eliminates all that mental turmoil of "should I, or should I not, go further." At this point, going forward is not a rational choice—it's your only choice.

When your search just keeps turning up dead ends, it can be extremely helpful to remember the caution that awakening is not an achievement. The journey consists of seeing through the false self. The awakening itself will likely be a huge—perhaps ecstatic—relief, but the preamble to awakening may drag you unmercifully through the dismal swamp of despair. It doesn't have to happen like that; it largely depends on how tightly you are trying to hold it all together. You don't really get to choose how it will all unfold. Life will do what it needs to do to wake you up out of your trance. And God doesn't always play nice.

As it says in the Introduction to *A Course in Miracles,* "This is a course in miracles. It is a required course. Only the time you take it is voluntary. Free will does not mean that you can establish the curriculum. It means only that you can elect what you want to take at a given time."

Maybe after being so honest about the potential difficulties of the journey, it is only fair to say that life after awakening is indeed better. Way better. I could go on to try to describe its wonders, but I'm sure you've read or heard the ads already: Peace, Bliss, Joy, etc. I know that "deep contentment" doesn't sound quite as alluring, but I assure you, deep contentment is very, very nice. There's also alleviation from that nagging sense of being separate from the rest of Life. And the stress and restlessness of seeking (in all its myriad forms) is transformed into the feeling of being at home in your own skin. And being released from the fear of death (not because of resignation or great courage, but rather, from the realization that death is another event, albeit a dramatic one, occurring in consciousness). This realization is an enormous relief and allows one to live life fully. So, yes, the view from awakeness makes pre-awakening seem like a life unlived no matter how exciting and rewarding it seemed at the time.

"Fine," you may say (remembering that mama

didn't raise no fool), "that sounds nice, but what is it going to cost me?" Well, if you are into this spirituality thing just to gain a new identity and feel a little better, then it doesn't really cost much of anything. However, if you are into this to "go all the way," then it will cost you everything.

Awakening is not an enhancement of you; it is a stripping away of everything you think you are. And sometimes that process is not pretty and may not be fun. If you are into the game for aggrandizement, you will be sorely disappointed, or you will drift into a self-induced, pseudo-spiritual fantasy. Or, if you are honest with yourself, you will quickly (or slowly) learn to get in alignment with how things actually are. It depends on your true motivation and your own innate integrity. No one can really help you there. You either have the capacity for self-honesty or you don't. Or, maybe suffering leaves you no other choice.

And if you follow the thread of truth with devotion and one day awakeness awakens to itself, *you* (as the awakeness that *you* are) will realize that awakening is not anything that you (as a separate imaginary being) could possibly take credit for.

How could recognizing what *you* already are, and have always been, be an achievement? When you recognize that the sought is that which is seeking, as Nisargadatta pointed out, the whole game of hide-and-seek collapses. It is often either slightly embarrassing or hilarious or both: embarrassing because you have spent so long looking for something so obvious, and hilarious because, well, it's the funniest practical joke ever played on us humans.

Let me ask this: When you graduated from high school, or you got your big career break, or learned a foreign language, or wrote the great American novel, did you feel embarrassed or incapacitated by laughter? Of course not! In achievement, there is a sense of accomplishment; some pride is excusable—you feel justly rewarded for your efforts. In awakening (once the sophomoric thrill of "Yeah! I'm awake!" wears off—hopefully very quickly), you come to realize that you will have accomplished absolutely nothing and that only by loss was anything truly gained. Any pride taken in awakening is delusional because, if the awakening is genuine, you realize that everyone else is already inherently awake. The only difference is that some folks know it; most don't. There is compassion for all; there is no sense of specialness.

When the Buddha awoke, he is reported to have said, "I and all beings have simultaneously awakened." This is how the story has been handed down to us, but that particular pronouncement, if true, probably occurred only after an hour or two of howling belly laughs at his years of deprivation in search of something so obvious and at the wonder of Maya's magic. However, those first few hours (or days) might have been a little too lighthearted to have made it into Buddhist scripture—or perhaps all those years of deprivation dulled his sense of humor. No one knows.

With achievement, you feel that the reward

is justified—paid for in full by your efforts, an even trade. With awakening, the "reward" is immeasurable and infinitely beyond any effort expended—no matter how hard and how long you spent seeking. There's no feeling of "Well, I earned that." There is no sense that the reward corresponds to the effort—even if it was forty years of effort. When you finally arrive home, there is only immense gratitude, delight, and a deep sense of unburdening.

So we hear about how wonderful awakening is, and so, logically, we set off in search of it. That's what seekers do until what is sought is found. Seeking isn't necessarily necessary, but people in the vicinity of the sphere of "spirituality" generally get caught in the gravitational effects of seeking.

The imagined goal of this search is unique for each person. It is often spoken about as seeking enlightenment (or God or Truth or Nirvana or Christ-Consciousness or Oneness or Wholeness or Reality or Buddha Nature or whatever else you choose to call it), but since enlightenment cannot be described or conceptualized, it will never be whatever you may think it will be. Therefore, you cannot actually seek enlightenment directly. You can seek only what enlightenment is falsely thought to be. Maybe enlightenment is imagined to be a perpetually high state, or a state with wonderful spiritual powers that we can use to wield influence in the world and to impress our friends, or we imagine there will be just a little peace of mind and an end to our personal problems, pain, and suffering.

Note: Maya, the Goddess of Illusion, does some of her best work here and will use whatever bait is necessary to get you to set out in search of *you*. You may not fully appreciate her talents now, but eventually, you will be deeply grateful for her skillful deceptions. Without the illusion of suffering or dissatisfaction, there would be no motivation to seek relief. The Goddess of Illusion uses illusion to dispel the trance of illusion. You have to marvel. Come on—give credit where credit is due!

Before awakening, almost unavoidably, you will believe that when you achieve enlightenment, you will be an enlightened being thereafter, which will be very impressive. People will notice you and respect you and be grateful for your presence, advice, and opinions, and your problems will vanish into the haze of perpetual bliss, and everything you do will be perfect because, well, because you are enlightened.

I hope you don't take this the wrong way, but "you," as you know yourself now, will never wake up. Never, ever. It's not just you. No *person* ever wakes up.

It is the One Consciousness that wakes up to Itself. It wakes up out of the dream of being fused with an individual bodymind that believes that it is somehow separate from the rest of Life.

You, as you have known yourself, are part of the trance. You believe you know what is real. You listen to voices in your head (thoughts) that you believe are true. You think you are a person that exists as a biological entity independent and separate from the rest of Existence. You think you were born and will die. You think the world would be a better place if everyone else would just listen to you. You believe that you are a woman (or a man). You believe that there was a Past and there will be a Future. You believe that there is a world out there and it's something you walk around in.

Not one of these beliefs is true. Not one!

You don't wake up to an exalted version of yourself because you don't actually exist as a separate entity in the first place. Fantasizing about a superior version of a nonexistent trance state doesn't even make any sense. It won't ever happen. This is what Buddhists mean when they talk about no-self. They don't mean a state that "you" as a little separate self can visit occasionally in meditation; they actually mean exactly what the term implies: there is no such entity as a separate self. You are not separate from existence. If this is the first time you've heard this news, it might be frightening, unbelievable, or just plain weird, but that is how Life is, and it is where your true home lies. *You* (as *you* really are) are the one spirit temporarily functioning as and through your mind/body unit (MBU). If you believe this statement as a philosophical assertion, it is of no real value. However, when the truth to which this statement points bursts forth in you, it transforms everything.

When consciousness wakes up to itself in a sustained way, only then is it possible for consciousness to penetrate the dream state without getting lost in it again. Then the dream state can be seen as just another aspect of the whole and not inherently separate from consciousness. Just as the dancer and the dance are inseparable. God is no longer imagined as a beingness *in* the world. The world we all see and walk around in *is* the creative manifestation of the One Consciousness and therefore indivisible from it. God is the world. Samsara and Nirvana are one. No separation. No distinction.

And you are already home—because there is nowhere else to go.

There is no future attainment to achieve. Everything is already fully present.

Awakening is not the end of the journey, but it is the end of seeking. It's like the corny grade school riddle: "When you are looking for your keys, why are they always in the last place you look?" The answer, of course, is that when you find your keys, you stop looking for them. After awakening, there is still movement and change, but it is more like God pulling you along rather than you having to slog your way uphill along a muddy path with only your limited personal willpower as motivation. After awakening, you can either resist further change or not, but the pull is inexorable, and the most you can do is postpone the inevitable. My recommendation is to let go and let it happen. Or you can resist and suffer. It's your choice.

When asked *how* to proceed at this point, David Hawkins, M.D., suggests relying on the acronym H.O.W., which stands for "honesty, openness, and willingness." These seemingly simple traits are essential.

At this stage of the journey to nowhere:

- remain alert
- be grateful for what has been realized, but not complacent
- let go more and more
- be open to change
- surrender the keys to your vehicle (your MBU, not your Chevy)
- get out of the way

and enjoy the journey that never ends.

Wheeee!!!

# Myth #1

"I Know What Awakening Will Look Like"

We've all read stories about mind-blowing awakening experiences. It makes good press. People who've had amazing, otherworldly, merging-with-all-things, expanding-to-the-limits-of-the-Universe awakening experiences are envied and admired. The seeker wants that. Who wouldn't?

What doesn't make front-page news, even though it's perhaps more common, is the simple seeing of our True Nature that is beyond all attributes, including those conjured up by the term "True Nature." This simple recognition may often be followed by mundane responses of complete surprise, like: "Could it really be that simple?" or "Why, that's been there all along. How is it possible I missed it?" or "Wow, that's not what I expected!" or, often, just uncontrollable belly laughter.

As you can imagine, the prospect of this less glamorous, but equally valid, form of awakening doesn't carry the same degree of fascination to our grasping minds. "Give me the mind-blowing flavor. Please!"

But, alas, you are not in Baskin-Robbins® and you don't get to choose. Awakening comes in whatever package it comes in. What you can do is not mistake the packaging for the gift. Gratitude is highly recommended regardless of the form in which the gift is delivered. No matter what form, or to what degree awakeness presents itself, be grateful for what is revealed.

Maybe there is just a glimpse. Wonderful. Receive the gift. Honor the gift. Allow it to be absorbed fully into your being. The immensity of the gift may not be immediately obvious. Give it the benefit of your attention. Give it time. Let the implications of the realization mature within you. Don't demand a home-run on your first date.

Finally, remember that all experiences come and go. Your awakening experience will not be an exception. Memorable for sure, but the experience itself will be impermanent, like all other events in your life. Experiences such as visions, altered states, energetic impulses in the body, and overwhelming bliss may be present concurrent with your awakening. All of these experiential occurrences will fade. Maybe not immediately, but eventually they will. The awakening itself may or may not fade. Don't mistake the experiential by-products for the awakeness. They are not the same thing.

Awakeness is not a peak experience and it is not a high state. It is our natural state, as the Taoist sages have told us. Awakeness is the field of consciousness within which all experiences and all states present themselves. The field of consciousness does not come and go. Consciousness is what is awake to all experiences: blissful experiences, mundane experiences, birth-life-death experiences, and everything in between. You *are* that awake presence. However, any attempt to hang on to that awareness or to the awakening experience itself will cause it to appear to slip from view.

"How can this be?" you may ask. "I thought that my awakening experience would be so powerful that I would be forever awake and thereafter reside in an eternal, blissful, altered state." This is similar to the line of reasoning diligently "researched" by the late Timothy Leary, which was basically, "If I get really high, and stay high enough for long enough, maybe I can stay high forever." It turns out, as Timothy sadly proved, that you just get goofy.

The myth about the imagined fireworks of awakening causes many people to miss the true significance of awakening moments when they do occur. Awakening can be accompanied by huge energy surges and an extraordinary cascade of realizations and images. The joy of recognition can be overwhelming. The sheer relief of it can be enormous. But all of these fireworks are not the awakeness itself. Fireworks may or may not be present when awakeness reveals itself to itself. The fireworks, if present, are by-products of waking up, not the awakeness itself. The by-products may be so fascinating and overwhelming that it may not be at all obvious that they are other than the awakeness. Here's how you can tell the difference: The by-products will fade into a memory of the experience; the awakeness, if it sticks, will not fade and will remain a living presence.

The risk of this myth that we already know what our enlightenment will look like is that we have come to believe that enlightenment will be a fantastic fireworks show. Maybe, maybe not. And even if your awakening experience is of the explosive variety, the key take-home point is not the fireworks but rather that which notices the fireworks. If we are focused on the fireworks, we will likely miss the real gift. We have all done it before when enlightenment has quietly presented itself. Often.

No matter how many times we've heard that we awake to what we already are, we cannot possibly imagine what that is until it happens for us. Therefore, our understandable bias is to miss what is most important. "So what to do?" My advice? Remember the transitory nature of all experience and drop any ideas of what your awakening will look like. Be open. Let go of what you think you know about enlightenment. Do not look to the mind to be the final judge of what is realized—anything of ultimate importance is beyond the mind's ability to understand.

If we are expecting something to look a certain way, we can easily miss it if it appears in a different form. Just ask any good magician. Our attention is directed one way, and the magician is doing something else. There's a wonderful short video clip on YouTube of two basketball teams passing the ball back and forth. You are asked to watch and count how many times the ball changes teams. So you focus on counting and watching the ball and fail to notice that someone in a gorilla suit enters the game and walks around among the players waving both arms. You may not notice something even this flagrant simply because your attention is directed elsewhere—even if it's just elsewhere on the same computer screen!

It's the same potential problem when you expect awakeness to look a certain way. If you are expecting fireworks, you can easily dismiss the quiet sort of awakening. You can encounter awakeness and dismiss it without even hesitating because, at first glance, it may look ordinary, not very exciting. After all, it's been there the whole time. I have even heard people say, "So what? What's so great about consciousness?"

You don't miss it because it is so obscure or complex or distant or extraordinary; you miss it because it is so obvious, simple, and ordinary.

Excitement, by the way, is vastly overrated in the enlightenment game.

Or, if you do get the awakening with fireworks, you may focus on the fireworks and fail to notice what is noticing the fireworks. In which case, you missed everything.

For just a moment, right now, allow yourself to relax. Let the objects within that consciousness (i.e., the input data streams from the seven senses: seeing, hearing, taste, touch, smell, thought, and bodily sensations) fall away. Are you still conscious? Even without being conscious of any specific thing, is consciousness still there? Is that ordinary, everyday, run-of-the-mill, always-been-there consciousness exciting to the mind? You may say, "Nothing special or unusual is happening. What's so spiritual about that?" You don't find what you think you should find, so you dismiss what is actually present and go off on another search seeking what you believe awakening will be, not realizing that you just dragged and dropped your own True Nature into the trash can of your expectations.

Or maybe you notice that quiet, objectless consciousness, but you react to it. It's not subject to your control. It's mysterious. You can't get a good look at it. You can't even describe it very well. It seems to have infinite depth. It may feel a little scary, perhaps even terrifying. You aren't sure what may be lurking there in the darkness; it is unfamiliar, unfathomable, beyond the capacity of the mind to understand. There can be a certain quality of absence or voidness—a "place" where the concept of "you" as you currently know yourself may be threatened. (By the way, let me interject here that Nirvana doesn't translate as a state of being really, really happy forever. Nirvana translates as "cessation," as used, for example, in the phrase "the cessation of you.") So you may sense a palpable, impending cessation, you get scared off, and you beat a hasty retreat for the nearest exit back into the house of mirrors that you are familiar with. Even if you are painfully familiar with it, at least it is familiar. The gateless gate appears to close. Another opportunity is lost—as it has been many times before. (But there is always this next moment!)

Or maybe you have had a glimpse, or a short

vacation, into the field of awakeness, and you tried to hold onto the experience. If the event was ecstatic, your every instinct wants to hold onto it. And then—all too soon—the experiential components begin to fade. So you grasp more, and they fade more quickly. When the fireworks flame out, which they inevitably will (whether minutes, hours, days or months later), it is easy to convince yourself that you have returned to a state of unawakeness. Enlightenment appears to have abandoned you. It is especially painful because you have tasted bliss and you don't imagine you could ever "lose" it. But now you believe you really know what awakeness looks like and you keep hoping for that same energetic, ecstatic experience to return. Some people wait years and years, hoping that it will return in exactly the same way. It never does. Why would it? You've already had that unique experience. Expecting a replay, you have your eyes transfixed on the memory of that past event and you miss consciousness presenting itself anew in every moment.

If you only pay attention to the fireworks, you miss the most valuable point. No, it's worse than that. You miss the entire point: All the fireworks (and everything else) are occurring within what *you* are. *You,* as *you* really are, are the conscious field within which, and as which, everything appears. (Of course, this statement, like all statements about Truth, is inherently false, but more true than most statements by virtue of it at least pointing towards what is true.)

So if you hang onto the attributes of the experience and fall into despair when they leave you, which they will, you may find yourself spending the next several decades trying to re-experience that awakening moment, waiting for exactly the same exact brand of fireworks to return. Don't laugh. Many people do exactly that. A replication of that experience will never return. If you are waiting for that particular movie to return to the theater, you will wait a long, long time. (Apparently, God doesn't do reruns.)

And you will miss the feast that the Divine is

serving up today.

One of the most useful pieces of advice I ever got was from Adyashanti, who warned that the only way to remain awake when awakening occurs is to avoid trying to hold onto it. It sounds like odd—if not downright poor—advice if you've never heard it before, but like many things on the spiritual path, what is true is upside down and backwards from what our minds would have us believe. Every instinct in us wants to hold onto the experience. It feels so familiar and obvious and good that we can't believe we could ever lose it. And then the sensations begin to fade. A few hours later, or the next day, or a couple of months later, we come down from our high state, and we despair. If we believe that the fireworks *are* the awakeness, it can feel like we have lost our enlightenment. That, folks, is a painful sensation. The awakeness itself, however, cannot be lost because it has never really been absent. It is only our ego that tries to hang onto the experience. Let it go! Trust Life!

Reality/awakeness/enlightenment/consciousness, whatever you choose to call it, is the only thing that exists, so it can never go very far! To retain it, you have to be willing to let it go. And welcome it when it returns and let it go again. Sometimes it's in the foreground; sometimes it's in the background. But never absent. Give it free rein. Notice that sometimes it is expanded and sometimes it is focused or contracted. You are not giving it permission to do so; you are simply aligning yourself with how it naturally moves—aligning yourself with the flow of Life. If you insist that Life look a certain way, you will miss its beauty, its nuances, its heartbeat.

Nothing real can be lost. At worst, awakeness can be obscured by your belief in its absence.

If you feel that you gained and then lost your awakeness, a better approach is to ask yourself, "How am I denying my awakeness at this moment?" If you ask instead, "What do I have to do to get it back?" you are back on the not-so-merry-go-round. *Doing something* to get awakeness back denies its presence and leads you away from what is eternally, unavoidably here.

Don't be afraid to let it go. Where could it possibly go anyway? It is only your own thoughts that can convince you that it has abandoned you. Look closely at whether those thoughts are really true. Is consciousness not already present right now? To be repetitively clear, I mean the consciousness that is animating your very own Mind Body Unit, and I mean at this exact (and every) moment. Like right now. And Now! AND NOW!!

Forget everyone else's stories of their awakening experiences. Yours, I promise, will not be like any of them. Imagining and hoping that it will be only gets in the way.

Just notice the ever-present, objectless consciousness. Discover its power for yourself. Allow it time to reveal itself fully. There is no need to imagine anything or believe anything anyone says about it. Trust your own direct experience. Don't grant your mind the power of being the final judge and jury on the subject of Truth. Truth is beyond the realm of the mind. Your mind will never understand it.

You can't conceptualize your way to Reality. You can't believe your way to Oneness. You can't pretend your way to Oneness. Just notice what is true for you and then follow that thread with complete earnestness and devotion.

This book is intended to help cure the ailment of unawakeness. Once the ailment is cured, you don't need to keep taking the meds. Get on with Life!

You are already what you are seeking.

Slow down and notice.

Explore your own beingness. You are already complete and whole.

It cannot be otherwise.

Because,

It is indeed all One.

Many Blessings to you on your journey home.

# About the Author

Don Oakley won the New England High School Swimming Championship in the 100-yard butterfly; dropped out of Princeton University five months before graduating; traveled overland across Asia when Muslims still liked Americans; hitch-hiked through Malaysia, Australia, New Zealand, and Fiji; paddled 600 miles down the Kazan River to the Arctic Circle; studied architecture in Boston; spent three years at an ashram in India; consulted as a licensed Civil Engineer and built affordable houses in Oregon; worked as a full-time volunteer for Adyashanti's Open Gate Sangha organization for two years and now serves as one of its Directors; and, in 1997, founded Well Being Foundation, an independent, non-profit, non-denominational organization now located in northeast Tennessee where he and his lovely wife Patty Bottari are Directors, full-time managers, and chief potwashers of the Well Being Conference Center located on 160 serene rural acres surrounded by the scenic Powell River in the middle of Heaven. *It's Time to Wake up Now: The Top Ten Myths that Can Hijack Spiritual Awakening* is his first book.

# Suggested Further Reading

### Adyashanti
*Falling into Grace: Insights on the End of Suffering; Resurrecting Jesus: Embodying the Spirit of a Revolutionary Mystic; Emptiness Dancing; True Meditation: Discover the Freedom of Pure Awareness; My Secret Is Silence: Poetry and Sayings of Adyashanti*

### Jed McKenna
*Spiritual Enlightenment, The Damnedest Thing; Spiritual Warfare; Theory of Everything, The Enlightened Perspective*

### Byron Katie and Stephen Mitchell
*Loving What Is: Four Questions That Can Change Your Life; A Thousand Names for Joy: Living in Harmony with the Way Things Are*

### Fred Davis
*The Book of Undoing: Direct Pointing to Nondual Awareness; Awakening Clarity: A Spiritual Sampler*

### Eckhart Tolle
*The Power of Now, A Guide to Spiritual Enlightenment; Stillness Speaks*

### John Prendergast
*In Touch: How to Tune In to the Inner Guidance of Your Body and Trust Yourself*

Ramana Maharshi
> *The Collected Works of Sri Ramana Maharshi*

Lao Tzu
> *Tao Te Ching*

Scott Kiloby
> *Living Realization: A Simple, Plain-English Guide to Non-Duality; Love's Quiet Revolution: The End of the Spiritual Search*

David Hawkins, M.D.
> *Discovery of the Presence of God: Devotional Non-Duality; Dissolving the Ego, Realizing the Self: Contemplations from the Teachings of David R. Hawkins*

Loch Kelly and Adyashanti
> *Shift into Freedom: The Science and Practice of Open-Hearted Awareness*

Steven Harrison
> *Doing Nothing: Coming to the End of the Spiritual Search; Getting to Where You Are; Being One*

Will Pye
> *Blessed with a Brain Tumor*

Nisargadatta Mararaj
> *I Am That*

Foundation for Inner Peace
> *A Course in Miracles*

Made in the USA
Columbia, SC
13 March 2019